CRIME FICTION

CRIME FICTION

*UEA MA
Creative Writing Anthologies
2020*

CONTENTS

WILLIAM SHAW	Foreword	VII
JULIA CROUCH	Introduction	IX
KATIE BEHAN	The Summer of Wasps	2
DENISE BENNETT	The Ravenous Tiger	18
LUCY DIXON	Scars	34
MARK HANKIN	Who Touches Me Is Broken	46
HELEN JONES	Broken English	62
LIN LE VERSHA	A Level in Murder	74
LISSA PELZER	The Personal Liar	88
AMANDA PERACCHI	An Off-Cut Murder	100
PAUL STONE	Number One	114
EMMA STYLES	No Country for Girls	128
MARTIN UNGLESS	Orange612	142
LUCY WOOD	Holloway	156
	Acknowledgements	171

WILLIAM SHAW
Foreword

Crime fiction is an extraordinary genre. It's one that doesn't know its place, and it never really has.

From the moment print technology made the sale of stories possible, printers found that grisly tales sold better. To the disgust of those who thought ink should be used only for self-improvement, it was obvious that murder ballads were what the readers really wanted. As one street ballad vendor told Henry Mayhew in the 1850s, 'There's nothing beats a stunning good murder, after all.'

There is a reason why crime fiction is still so loved, and why the writers featured in the following pages are telling the stories we want to hear. The human appetite for the grisly is an entirely natural one. Blood, cruelty and deception lie behind the oldest stories we've been told.

Crime writers have always explored this indecent fascination, but as the genre evolved it has, I think, acquired much greater power. In this safer and less credulous age, writers like the ones you're about to read have had to work much harder than those ballad writers to make us believe in the horror of violent death.

The best post-war crime fiction was about world-building. In a few brilliant words Simenon could transport you to a bar on the Seine that you absolutely knew was real; the drink a character chose, marc or milk or calvados, would define his or her place and opinions. From that place, he could convince you of the grisliest murder. In Britain, writers like P D James, Ruth Rendell and Reginald Hill resonated because of their deft observations of character and place, of social nuances. Having placed the crime into this very real world, the act of detection itself began to change. Whether by accident or design, crime fiction evolved into a kind of forensic examination itself. Writers find themselves exploring our society, our politics and our relationships.

Writers like Val McDermid and former UEA UNESCO Visiting Professor Ian Rankin aren't just solving murders; their detectives are investigating a moral and social universe. As Ian wrote in the foreword to a previous edition of this book, 'If I want to know about a nation, I will read its crime fiction.' It was no coincidence that the #MeToo movement and psychological fiction appeared at the same time; crime writers were already finding new ways to tell stories about domestic abuse and the power relationships that are hidden behind closed doors.

If crime fiction now dominates our storytelling culture, topping the book charts and filling the television schedules, it's because it strikes a chord in the way it occupies this extraordinary ground, this uneasy and yet powerful place between fiction and non-fiction. And in that sense as well, it's a genre that doesn't know its place. The horrors and cruelties it depicts might be imaginary, but its writers convince you they are real by the quality of their insight and observation about everything else that surrounds them.

Which makes it all sound very worthy and serious. But the impulse behind writing it is just the same as was, I presume, behind those murder ballads. Above all, these writers create stories to entertain. The rest is extra. There's nothing beats a stunning good murder, after all.

JULIA CROUCH
Introduction

This is the third year I have been associated with the UEA Crime Writing MA course and, once again, I am deeply impressed by the diversity and quality of the writing produced by our students.

Crime writing is a broad church. Far from being just about cops and robbers, violence, action and entertainment, at its best it holds a mirror up to our world, urging us to examine the line between right and wrong, and what leads people to cross it. The best crime fiction leans into the darkest and the noblest parts of humanity, and can take us into all areas of society – from inner-city council estate to remote Greek island, from outwardly innocent English suburbia to raw, Australian outback. You'll find all of that in here, and more.

This is a demanding course. The bar for entry is high, the amount of work and commitment expected great. But it needs to be like that, because writing a novel is no easy enterprise. Yes, you need talent, skill, craft, imagination and determination to the point of bloody-mindedness. But you also need to be able to evaluate your work critically, to see it in the context of other writing, so that you can figure out, from premise to plot to paragraph, what works and what doesn't. This is where this course comes into its own. Through detailed tutor and peer feedback, UEA Crime Fiction writers gain the support and skills they need for taking their novel from bright idea to a refined and considered 65,000-plus words – extracts from which are now within these pages.

All novelists experience anxiety and/or self-doubt. This is generally felt most acutely during the writing of the difficult middle section – the part where the transition of the perfect novel of your dreams into something more flawed and real can cause you to question the whole project. It is also the part where many beginner writers lose heart and give up. This course provides students with professional tuition and feedback. But also, crucially, it makes a space – real and virtual – to share problems and celebrate successes with peers, thereby fostering the ability to acknowledge these difficulties, and to develop strategies for overcoming them.

This year has not been without its challenges – Lockdown has meant that we have all had to find new ways of working. However, this course could have been built for such circumstances. With students coming from all over the world, with all sorts of home and work responsibilities and commitments, the emphasis has always been on flexibility, and much of the one-to-one teaching is normally done remotely, through online tools and video conferencing. For the spring residential, we have even scheduled a virtual pub evening, so that the all-important social side of the course – every writer needs a network – isn't entirely lost. It's not quite a night on the tiles in Norwich, but the conversation will be just as good.

So, here's to the class of 2020, working in their makeshift studies all over the world – from kitchen table to tarted-up garden shed, from ergonomic home office to sofa strewn with children's toys – to produce the novels you are getting just a taste of here. The journey of the past two years is coming to an end. The journey has just begun.

This diverse anthology comprises the latest work from the 2020 cohort of crime fiction writers studying UEA's renowned Creative Writing MA.

KATIE BEHAN

Katie Behan earns her living temping in offices. Prior to this she worked in social care and before that she was a TEFL teacher in Japan. She also writes comedy and has written content for BBC Radio Four, Radio Four Extra and BBC Comedy Scotland. This is her first novel.

Bridgetburgoyne1@gmail.com

The Summer of Wasps

CHAPTER ONE

My head felt tangled. I had ten minutes till my appointment, so I walked up Camden High Street. Tinsel in shop windows. Stars hanging from streetlights.

A charity shop; nothing worth buying, just a musty smell. Coldplay's *Christmas Lights* on the radio then the news. Unemployment stats were up, homelessness was unprecedented and a famous director, James Russo, was missing. He'd been filming in London. Some comic book franchise and he'd disappeared in the middle of a scene. Hollywood was up in arms. BAFTA was having a seizure and various actors were heartbroken. I spotted a paisley scarf on the way out, but it felt scratchy. Left without it. Kept on walking.

Past a mongrel tied to a lamppost, lying on the ground, surrounded by North London busy and too bored to even bark.

'Cheer up.'

He didn't want to.

Outside the World's End pub. Opposite Camden Town Tube. Commuters everywhere, free papers being handed out, musicians gifting their CDs to anyone who'd take one.

And him.

Tall. Neat. Cashmere coat.

Black leather satchel over his shoulder.

A jittery feeling of sickness. It's work, I told myself, that's all. That's why he's asked to meet. But my palms still sweated in the early evening chill.

He saw me. Ran across the road. Touched my chin. Rough hands. Nails bitten to the quick. Gaunt face, shadows and torn lips.

'Has something happened, Ollie?'

He checked his phone. 'First wine.'

I nearly asked him back to my bedsit, but then remembered the last time we'd been together. An accidental meeting by the village hall, after my nan's wake. That night. Whispers. Him telling me that everything was going to be OK. Touching my body and kissing my tears. I prayed he'd never let me go.

The next morning, after he'd gone, when I was curled up in the shower and drenched in water, I realised it was the worst thing that could have happened. All I'd wanted was kindness; sweet, simple.

Fifteen minutes later we were in a cheap backpackers' pub that smelt of wet dog. Mostly Australians, talking loudly, excited and guzzling alcohol in two-pint glasses while they played pool. My age, except I felt about a hundred and ten.

Ollie looked round and then tried to disappear into the collar of his jacket.

'Snob.'

'I'm not, Lily, this place is bloody awful.'

He put his phone on the table. 'Even the World's End would have been better.'

'You said I could choose.'

'I regret every word.'

I watched him peer at a guy in a Roxy beanie. Ollie always looked at people as if they smelt. In fairness though, woolly hat man did. The canine odour was entirely his creation.

Then silence. I touched the table. Dirty, sticky. My hand, when I sniffed it, was a hundred percent 'quantity not quality' beer. Someone put an old rock song on the jukebox. *Living on a Prayer*, Bon Jovi. Ollie gnawed at his finger and stared at me. One of us had to do something so I reached for his hand.

'What is it? What's wrong?'

He stroked my wrist with his thumb. Gentle, rhythmic. 'Missed you, pretty girl.'

'Stop it.'

'I'm sorry.'

Alsatian boy shuffled past. The juggling of pool cue and cider was too much for him and he slopped booze onto Ollie's shoulder. The Ollie I knew would have had a hissy fit; the one I was with barely noticed.

'It's about Sam,' he said.

I leant forward. 'Is he OK?'

'I don't think so.'

We made eye contact. I looked away. 'Explain.'

He took a gulp of wine. 'Christ, this drink is awful. OK, so, you know the band She Walks in Beauty?'

'Yeah.'

'Well, Sam's started hanging around with the singer.'

'Tristan Burnett? Really? Wow, but he's...'

'A car crash. Yeah.'

'I was going for a great musician, but OK, that too.' I paused for a second. 'Sam didn't say anything in July.'

He studied me. His expression unreadable. 'He said you'd met.'

'That's because we met.'

His brother and I went way back, and I wasn't in the mood for any weirdness about it. I made a face and Ollie rolled his eyes at me.

'Anyway, he's only known Tristan a few months. The guy goes to open mic nights, apparently. Just turns up, dazzles everyone with that handful of nineties hits.'

'Sam was playing?'

'Yeah, a pub near Turnpike Lane. The Chelsea. Tristan loved his music, invited him back to his place and that was that. A new member of his entourage.' His voice tightened. 'Sam's been full of it. Tristan loves my music. Tristan thinks I've got a good vibe.'

'A good vibe, who even says that?'

Ollie smiled. Draped his arm across the chair next to him.

'Sam's even dated one of his...' he paused and made inverted commas with his fingers, '...friends. I met her. Daisy. Absolute nutter. Spent the night talking in haikus.'

He crossed his legs. His shoes were black suede. Pristine.

I sipped my drink. 'If she could have picked one person not to quote poetry at.'

'It was horrific. I mean I like Japanese poetry as much as the next guy, hang on a minute. Actually, no I don't.'

'Truthfully you probably do. I mean look around.'

One of the backpackers was standing on a table at the other side of the bar singing the Slade Christmas classic, jeans round his ankles, Santa boxers showing. A crowd of girls cheering him on.

'Christ,' Ollie said, 'this place is ghastly.'

'I like it. It's fun.'

A girl by the bar vomited on a chair. Ollie raised his eyebrows.

'Shut up.'

It was nice between us. For that minute.

'At least Sam's mixing with the right people. It's not what you know, it's who you know, and all that.'

He snorted, 'Tristan Burnett? The right people?'

'It might lead to opportunities.'

'Drugs, freakshow parties, odd sex, strange rumours, never washing, a sense of sordid debauchery. Those the opportunities you're referring to?'

'You know I'm going to have to tell all the other CEOs you're only pretending to read the *Financial Times*, secretly you're addicted to gossip.'

'You're not funny.'

'I am, though.'

A brief smile before he continued. 'And the weirdness, the guy is seriously fucking strange. I read an old interview where halfway through he starts speaking in tongues.'

'Drugs? An image thing? Anyway, Sam's an adult, he can hang around with whoever he wants. I don't get why you're so worried.'

Ollie grabbed his mobile from the centre of the table. Fiddled with it. Handed it to me.

'I got this two days ago.'

The voice message kicked in. A robotic sounding woman. 'Message received Wednesday the twentieth-eighth of November at four thirty.'

Ollie stared over my shoulder. Sam's voice, hesitant, soft and familiar. Slight lilt at the end of his words. A guitar playing in the background.

'It's me.'

A long pause, like he wasn't going to speak again. Then he spoke quickly.

'Sorry I've been... I've not been around. There's been this situation, you see,' his voice started breaking, he took a breath, jagged and deep. 'Ollie, they've done something bad, really bad... and I don't know what to do.'

The music stopped. A few seconds of Sam crying. Then he hung up.

Ollie still wouldn't look at me.

For a second the people round us were too big. Like giants.

The bar was fetid. Sweaty. But I was freezing.

Downed the rest of my wine.

'I was in a meeting when he rang. Some bollocks that could have waited.'

'You've called him back?'

'Goes straight to voicemail.' Ollie leant across the table. Clutched my arm. 'Listen to it again, to the noise in the background.'

'I don't need to.' I put the phone on the table. 'It was a She Walks in Beauty song, Tristan singing. But they split up years ago?'

'Yeah, late nineties. Just after the lead guitarist died of a drugs overdose. The bassist bought a mansion in Norfolk and rebranded himself, he's now a farmer, and the drummer is a trance DJ in Australia.'

'Didn't know you were a fan too?'

'Funny. I got the info off the internet, bloody obviously.'

'So, we need to know if Tristan is gigging by himself, unplugged style. He might have been rehearsing. Sam might be with him?'

He gave me a strange look. 'I'm not in your line of work, but neither am I an idiot. There's nothing listed anywhere.' He stood up. 'I'm getting more of whatever the hell it is they're calling wine.'

I got my purse out, but he waved me away. Buying us a bottle would have left me broke for a few days. But I'd have done it.

I thought of Sam, our London meet-up had been disastrous. Pizza in a cheap chain pub, designed to look like the bar in the old American sitcom where everybody knew your name. I'd only been in the city two weeks. Nobody knew my name. And years of being a carer for my nan back in our hometown while Sam had enjoyed himself in London had left us mismatched. I had no stories. No conversation. He rambled about needing to find his purpose, his truth through music and it left me cold and annoyed. He spent so much time stressing about his existence. All that wasted space. Sam could have filled that space with anything. I hated that he hadn't. He hadn't in all those years that I couldn't.

Then I remembered him as a teenager. Playing guitar, singing. Writing songs. Telling me the latest facts he'd learnt about whatever random thing he was obsessed with. Never fully aware of the effect he had on other people. Ignoring their laughter when he said something weird. It was almost as if he didn't hear them. *Almost*.

I should have stayed in better touch. Answered his texts. Met him for coffee. Wasn't sure why I hadn't. But I realised, sitting there, surrounded by pissed-up travellers singing *This Is Me* from *The Greatest Showman* that I missed my childhood friend. Very much.

'So, I was wondering,' Ollie said when he returned with Pinot Grigio, 'whether your firm would look for Sam?'

So that really was the only reason for our meeting. Even though he'd been there in my darkest hour. Wrapped round me. While the weather lashed against the window. I kept poker faced.

'Absolutely. Consider it a case taken on,' I said with the authority of someone who had the power to make those decisions.

He poured us both a glass. Then downed his. 'What is the name of the firm? Sam never said.'

'F Investigations.'

'Is there a website?'

'No.'

'Right.' He paused. Confused. 'What are your rates?'

I put on my most 'business-like' voice. 'We'll sort that out with you next week.'

I had no idea, but I wasn't going to tell him that.

I'd told Sam, when we'd met up, that I had a job with a private investigation firm. He was impressed.

'Awesome! Like in a movie?'

'Yes. Exactly like that.'

I changed the subject before he could ask me anything else.

'I'm going to ask you some questions now, Ollie.'

He sat upright.

'When was the last time you saw Sam?'

'That's very good. You sound awfully professional.'

I stuck my tongue out. He smiled.

'I'm serious. You do. OK. So, he and I meet for dinner every third Thursday,' he downed, 'we've done that for the last five years. Since he moved here as a matter of fact. I like to keep a check on him, see if he needs any money. If he's eating his vegetables, that kind of thing.'

We sat in silence for a few seconds. The crowd were singing along to The Pogues, *Fairytale of New York*. Not a sober eye in the house. I drunk some more wine. Keen to join them.

Ollie bit at his knuckles, then carried on. 'He's missed the last two. He's been avoiding my calls. I wasn't happy about it, but I just thought... well, I don't know what I thought.' He laughed, wry and harsh. 'He was enjoying the rock 'n' roll life, I guess.'

'Were you jealous? Worried he'd have a turn in the sun for a change?'

He stared at me. 'Jesus, Lily, where did that come from?'

I shrugged. I'd thought it, so I'd said it. He rubbed his hand through his hair. Made it messy.

'Sam's problems were never my fault, OK? Sometimes brothers don't get on, you wouldn't get that because you're an only child. And, for the record, I wasn't in charge of what our parents thought, and I didn't bloody well get into private school to spite him. Or into Oxford.'

Or into my bed. But I didn't say that out loud.

A slight plea in his voice, a rawness that I'd never heard before. I didn't know what to do with it, so I carried on gathering facts. 'Is he still working in the record shop?'

'No, it closed a few months ago. I was putting money into his account, so he could focus on his music. *That's* how much I care.'

All right Ollie, I thought, I get it. The past between you is cancelled, and the only dynamic that matters is the one you have now. Except life doesn't work like that.

I coughed, professionally, and ploughed on. 'Is he still living in the same house?'

'No. I went to see his landlady this morning. She said he moved out weeks ago.'

'Where is he living now?'

'No idea.'

I took a couple of gulps of wine. Ollie got up. Sat next to me instead of opposite. Kissed my cheek. 'It might be nothing. Just my brother getting worked up.'

'You don't think that.'

'No, I don't.'

He stroked my arm and rested his head on my shoulder. I wanted so badly to lean into his touch. He kissed my cheek again. I turned. We were inches away from each other. His breathing got heavier.

I looked at his left hand. 'How's your fiancée?'

His expression changed. For a second, I thought he was going to cry. But that was my imagination, it must have been.

'I'm so sorry...'

'She still doing well at life?'

He whispered into my ear. 'There's something about you. I think about you all the time, even when I'm with Hannah. Especially when I'm with her...'

'Whatever.'

'You know I'd leave her for you, don't you?'

Then a rage so great that I could have smashed my glass on the floor and screamed. Instead I pushed him away. Hard.

'Lily, please, the last time we saw each other, I shouldn't have...'

'Doesn't matter.'

'You were grieving, and I was wrong to... it was all my fault. I'm so sorry.'

'Are you? That's big of you. To be so very sorry.'

I didn't realise I was shouting, till two of the backpackers turned and stared.

That night, the one after Nan was buried, the sex with him had been delicate and safe. A refuge. For a few hours anyway. And then, months later, it was just apologised for.

Great.

I wiped my eyes, quickly and efficiently. What the hell was I doing?

He got up, 'We should go.'

Slight rain and the streets were oddly empty for a Friday night in Camden. We were both unsteady on our feet but didn't touch. We parted on the corner closest to my place. Near us, a fox sniffed round a takeaway box. We watched it for a second. Bold and mangy. I kicked the pavement by Ollie's toe. The animal glared at me. Then carried on scavenging.

'If you're about to apologise again I swear to God, I won't be responsible.'

He held his hands up in mock surrender. 'I wouldn't dare!'

I smiled. He grinned back, lopsided. I wanted to step into his arms. Have him kiss my neck. And then punch him as hard as I could.

'Goodnight Ollie.'

I crossed the road. Stood in front of my door. Felt him watching.

'Lily?'

I turned.

'I love my brother, you know that?'

I didn't answer.

'I'd never begrudge him anything.'

Kept silent. Should have reassured him, but his discomfort was giving me a vicious stab of pleasure.

A few beats then he walked away. Back towards the Tube. A crowd of drunken women whooped as they skittered past. Cold bare legs. Linked arms and mangled carols. He kept going.

Tall. Neat. Cashmere coat.

Black leather satchel over his shoulder.

The fox was still there when I stepped inside. Staring. Chicken carcass in its jaws.

CHAPTER TWO

Mattress, fridge, sink, kettle, radio, chest of drawers, cloth wardrobe, hob, cat litter tray, cat tree. My bedsit.

Morrison, the grey tabby I'd inherited from my nan wasn't impressed with my lateness.

'Sorry.'

I retrieved her cloth mouse from under my pillow and wriggled it along the mattress. She licked her tail and ignored me.

Sometimes, in the early hours of the morning I'd take her outside on a lead. The foxes had become a problem. At first, they ran off when I shouted, but their numbers had increased along with their confidence. They scared her. A strange growling sound that she'd never made before.

She belonged in the village. Fields. Lanes where she could roam. Where the foxes kept to themselves. The day I moved to London I left her with neighbours, but she yowled and scratched their furniture. They begged me to take her back. The second we were reunited, she was quiet. Two hours later, on the coach, Morrison next to me in her purple carrier, I watched everything we knew fade into the distance.

'Food!' She loved that word. Tea gobbled, peevishness forgotten, we walked about the building. A falafel restaurant took up the ground floor, but the top one was all ours. Three empty bedsits and a hallway. Paint-peeled walls and matted carpet. Metamorphosis was on the horizon. Shiny, overpriced and generic. The property developers were only waiting for the lease on the Lebanese place to run out. Our presence, at greatly reduced rent, was supposed to keep the building safe.

I turned the hall light off so we could look at the tiny glowing stars I'd stuck to the ceiling.

'Aren't they nice, Morrison?'

Her concentration was carpet based. Specifically, on the spider she was battering with her paws.

Half an hour later I realised that I was fully drunk. Not the sort where the room spins but the kind that throws out random thoughts. A scatty overdrive that makes you dizzy. I lay down, eyes shut, hoping, if I wished hard enough that I might sleep. Nice dreams. Backpackers singing. Talking about their travels. I loved that place. A flow of different people who knew nothing about me and cared even less. But my mind had designs on the past.

The first time I met Sam and Ollie, Ollie was thirteen, Sam and I three years younger. Some theatre group that my nan made me attend.

'It'll be good for you to mix. There are some lovely children around.'

'If they're so lovely, you go.'

She gave me a sandwich, kissed me and then threw me to the wolves.

All the other kids knew who I was. Who my dad was. I sat on the edge of the stage wishing the day was ending rather than starting. A boy appeared in front of me. Skinny, small, messy brown hair, orange jumper even though it was July. He smelt of strawberry chews.

'What?' I asked him.

'Did you know that polar bears are really curious? So, if you think you are going to get attacked by one, it's really good because all you have to do is throw something on the ground like a handkerchief or, if you haven't got one of those, a tissue.'

'How would I know that?'

He shrugged.

I asked again. 'How would anyone know that?'

A few feet away from us three girls and a boy were laughing. One of the girls crept towards us. Her lips dripped gloss; her mouth smacked gum.

'The polar bear will stop to look at...'

She started speaking.

'The polar bear will stop to look at...'

She'd made her voice high and gentle in mimicry. The boy's left eye started to twitch slightly.

'It just gives you time to...'

'It just gives you time to...'

Every time he spoke, she did her imitation. Always a few words in the drag. The friends behind her were hysterical. The older lad especially. With his top-of-the-range skateboard gear. The entertainment only stopped when the youth worker came into the room.

'Now, get into pairs.'

I told the boy he could work with me and he beamed from ear to ear, like it was the best news he'd ever had. Slipped his damp hand into mine.

Later, in our biscuit and lemonade break, I asked him why he was wearing a woollen jumper.

'Because it's my favourite.'

'But you're sweating.'

'It's still my favourite though.'

It was a logic I couldn't argue with.

Skater boy and his groupies sneered at us from a distance. My new friend saw me looking.

'That's my brother Ollie and his friend Hannah.'

'Do you think we should throw a handkerchief on the ground?'

The boy looked serious. 'It only works on bears.'

Then another memory. My eleventh birthday. A bright June day. The ice-cream parlour in the nearest town. Dad eating a cone and laughing loudly while my nan stroked his arm.

I watched them. My sundae melted. Then we waved him off to London on the coach.

Nan held my hand. 'Just you and me again, love.'

I felt a bit dazed, like the sun from that day was shining in my eyes.

I sat up. 'None of this.'

Checked an address on my phone, then slung some clothes on.

'Poppet,' I kissed the purring cat, 'I'm on a case.'

A night bus to Turnpike Lane. Rowdy passengers. Christmas cheer. I spent the journey calling Sam and getting his voicemail. Didn't bother to leave a message.

The Chelsea pub. Off Greenlanes. Big Turkish and Kurdish communities. Good, cheap restaurants. Cafés. A nice feel to the place. The odd bistro; gentrification was creeping in, but it had a fight on its hands.

Smokers gathered round the pub, like a moat round a castle. Fingers dripping roll-ups. Cigarettes laced with the sweet scent of grass. The building was big. Solid. Detached. Glistening red wall tiles. Smooth and wet to the touch, like ironed rain. Flowerpots hung near the entrance, a tendril of something that was once alive snaked out of one.

But no Sam.

Inside, my eyes were drawn to the bar. Huge and circular it sat in the middle of the space and the rest of the pub happened round it. Two staff served. Behind them sat bottles of spirits, boxes of crisps and jars of children's sweets; lurid coloured gummy bears, dolly mix and midget gems. A display of cupcakes looked like they'd wandered into the place by accident. A mounted stag's head stared down from the bar wall, red tinsel woven through its antlers. The carpet was nineteen seventies style tatty, swirling yellow circles set in a murky purple. Old gnarled dressers, junk shop bookcases, knackered looking tables.

Various framed album covers adorned the walls: Suede's *Dog Man Star*, *New Wave* by The Auteurs, *Spooky* by Lush, Blur's *Modern Life is Rubbish*. It was like the nineties had thrown up.

The pub had an 'antique chic' look that was painfully cultivated. But at the same time it was genuinely neglected. The smell of dust and old beer.

There was your general 'Friday night meets Saturday morning' chatting, but there was an edge. Too much looking around. People weren't 'living the moment', instead they were assessing how they fitted into it, ready to alter in some way, should that be required.

I'd never felt comfortable in places that demanded a performance.

Did a circle of the floor. Nobody I knew.

Music. A track I recognised, because my dad liked it. *Lithium* by Nirvana. I started to feel sad. Where was Sam?

What sort of song was that to play at Christmas time?

My drunk was turning bad. It needed feeding.

The bartender had a French accent with a hint of cockney. Light pink hair with an undercut and blue, heavily kohled, eyes. Lumberjack shirt and baggy jeans. The nineteen fifties-style name badge on her breast told me her name was Viv.

I yelled at the silver stud in her chin, 'Jack D and coke. Double.'

It appeared I was spending my food allowance on alcohol so I might as well go all out. 'And crisps.'

'What sort?'

'Salted.'

'Yeah, what sort?'

'The potato kind.'

Jesus, how many sorts were there. The crisps she gave me were nearly as expensive as the drink.

Asked her if she knew a guy called Sam.

'I know loads of guys called Sam.'

'You've been a great help. Thanks.'

I wandered over to a tall table. Stood and crunched my oddly bland snack. Felt her watching me.

One group a couple of tables away attracted my attention. Five men and two women. The former all morphed into one longish haired, oddly Victorian looking scruffy mass, but the women were interesting. The shorter one had bobbed auburn hair. Petite features. Nineteen nineties-style baby-doll dress. Fishnet tights and clumpy army boots. The taller one was model-skinny, blonde, and dressed in a nineteen twenties flapper outfit.

I looked down at my jeans, hoodie and duffel coat combo. Was everybody in this city in some kind of fashion-based time warp except me?

Red hair stood on the table, did some poses and the others clapped. A poem without words, she screamed and then jumped down. She was clearly under the influence, but then they all were. Movements slightly jarred and slow. She did a little turn, then curtseyed. Ollie would have thought they were a bunch of weirdos. A poem without words? It would have sent him over the edge.

Then I noticed that most of the pub was watching them. All the smokers who entered threw sneaky glances. Most of the people around gave the odd look over. Red was aware of the attention and played to it. Something about the way she held herself wasn't quite on the level. Like a bad actor playing to an audience she thought she'd never have.

They moved to an alcove. Animated chat, all except Red who sat with a blank expression.

I walked back over to the bar keeping as much of an eye on them as I could. No idea why I'd become fixated, guessed it was because Ollie had said Sam's girlfriend Daisy liked poetry. Wondered if it was her.

I ordered another double. A weekly food shop was for losers. Apparently, I could survive on air and bits of leftover cat food.

Viv slammed some change into my hand.

'Are you sure you haven't seen my friend Sam? He's about six foot, skinny, brown hair. Friends with Tristan Burnett.'

Something shifted in Viv's eyes and her colleague, who was making a gin for a man with a bushy beard, looked at me for a second before carrying on with her task. Viv covered her reaction with another dose of hostility.

'Move away from the bar – people are waiting.'

'Great customer service,' I said before retreating to the same table. Downed my drink in three gulps. Alcohol was smashing, I decided. Resolved to ingest more of it whenever I could.

I tuned into the music for a second. A track from The Cure's *Disintegration* album. Someone really needed to teach this place about Christmas.

A couple of minutes later the other bar woman was at my table. Her name badge said 'Elif – Manager'. She handed me some money.

'Your drink is on the house.'

I hesitated. 'Why?'

'Viv shouldn't have been grumpy with you, baby, but we're tired, down two members of staff.'

I put her at mid-forties. Beautiful green eyes. Olive skin. Voice like a docker that smoked forty a day.

'So, do you know Sam? I just need to talk to him.'

She smiled. Shook her head. Liar I thought, big, blatant, liar. Tried another tack.

'Tristan Burnett *does* drink here, doesn't he?'

The smile disappeared and her eyes didn't shift from mine.

'Why are you asking?'

'He's a friend.'

'Is he now?' She rested her elbows on the table.

'Absolutely. We've lost touch. Has he played a gig here recently?'

'No baby, because, despite the décor, it isn't the mid-nineties.'

'But he drinks here, right?'

'Rarely. My advice?' She pointed at me. 'Stay away from that man.'

Wondered if she was going to provide a reason that expanded on the tabloid rumours. Instead she put her mouth close to mine. Her breath tickled my lips. I looked down and noticed her nails were painted black.

'Why? What's so bad about him?'

'Everything. I don't know who you are but hanging around with rock royalty isn't what it's cracked up to be. Most of this lot,' she gestured at the customers, 'would kill to hang out with him. Or they think they would. Baby?'

'Yeah?'

'You ever been in a situation you thought you could handle, then it turned out you couldn't?'

I threw out a 'perhaps' in response. But I knew I had. Plenty of times. Just not in the way she meant. She winked then walked away. Tight black jeans. Celtic tattoos up her arms. The Velvet Undergound's Banana on the back of her T-shirt.

I sipped two more Jack Daniels. Did a couple more recces of the pub. Still no Sam. Ran my hand over the top of one of the cabinets, uneven and rough. Gave me a splinter.

DENISE BENNETT

Denise Bennett is a doctor who has worked in hospital and general practice. She recently returned to university and graduated in English Literature. Her first novel, a retelling of *Titus Andronicus*, melds her loves of Shakespeare and crime fiction. Denise lives near Guildford with her husband, her sons and too many pets.

denisebennett@me.com

The Ravenous Tiger
— *A retelling of Titus Andronicus*

CHAPTER ONE

A nobler man, a braver warrior,
Lives not this day within the city walls.
    —William Shakespeare, *Titus Andronicus*, 1.1.25

London, October 12, 2029

Detective Chief Superintendent Tina Andrews picked up her gun. A body had been found in Red Zone 13 – more than a routine stabbing by the sound of it. She slid the Glock Gen9 into her belt, grabbed her jacket, and went to round up a team.

The Central Elite hub was too quiet. Soft murmurs replaced the usual buzz of voices, interrupted only by the half-hearted tapping of computer keyboards. Even the phones observed a mournful silence.

'I want your attention,' she said. Thirty-four screen-bleached faces lifted to hers. 'City East have asked for our assistance in Red Zone 13.'

'Ma'am—'

'Rana?'

'It's Tommy's funeral today.'

There was a collective sigh.

'I'm aware,' said Tina, her voice tight, 'but until DS Ryan's coffin arrives at the church at four o'clock you've got a job to do.'

Rana shrank back into her seat.

Tina scanned the room. 'Luke. You're with me.'

'*You're* taking it, chief? I could do it, I'm due a big one,' he said.

She ignored him, turning to her office manager. 'Marcus, book out two ARVs for Brickfield Road E3, please. Set up an incident room, hotlines, drone-cam desk, the whole lot.'

'Yes, boss. Only...' Marcus's customary wicked grin was missing.

'Only?'

'You've got the Appeals Court meeting at 2pm.'

'I've got nearly five hours of freedom then.'

'Indeedy you do, boss.' The grin was back.

She searched faces; found those she wanted. 'DS Mütter, you lucky man. And Rana. You're both in the other ARV.'

Tina shivered in the cold, dank air of the Barbican's underground car park. Her armed response vehicle was ready, a German SUV with high-level ballistic protection – standard procedure for all call-outs to the city's red zones. She tossed the keys to Luke and settled herself into the passenger seat. The guards stood to attention, hands cradling their machine guns. One of them stepped into Silk Street to check the road was clear. Luke didn't wait, pulling out past the army tank situated at the main entrance to Barbican House. Their ARV almost clipped the guard, and narrowly missed a squad car that was turning in.

'Mmm. Like that is it?' Tina said.

'Fucking tank always stuck there on that blind bend. Non-operational piece of junk. They should dump it.'

'Deterrent, Luke. Reminds people of the bad old days.'

'Not like the unwashed masses are allowed down Silk Street though, is it?'

'True. But TV cameras are.'

He grunted.

'So... the finders are two kids. They phoned an ambulance,' Tina said.

'What, for the corpse?'

'No. One of them got sick, asthma attack I think. Paramedics called it in.'

'What were they doing in a red zone?'

'Probably the same as kids have always done. Smoking a spliff, hanging out. Getting away from adults.'

He nodded, then cursed. 'Gonna hit the start of the march, chief.'

'Shit. I forgot about the bloody march. Can you go round?'

'Not till we get to Finsbury Square.'

Two minutes later they were stuck behind a gaggle of early birds walking in the road, self-righteously oblivious to traffic. Their banners read: 'No to Death Penalty' and 'End this savagery' and 'Support Amnesty NOW!' Luke hammered the horn. Most of the marchers shuffled to the pavement. A young woman with long, blue dreadlocks turned to face them, mulish feet planted square in the way. Her sign pictured a severed head, blood dripping.

Tina heard her unspoken accusation, whispered on the web, that the police rounded up randomers in the street and sent them for execution.

Luke bashed a button on the dashboard, the loudhailer crackled into life, then... phut... nothing. 'Fancy foreign piece of shit,' he muttered, sliding down his window. 'Oi! You! Get out of the road before I arrest you for obstructing a police officer!'

Blue dreadlocks sauntered off and flipped the finger as they drove past.

'Fucking Public Order committee,' he said.

'Fucking what about it?' She'd been on the committee.

'Letting people march like this again. Why?'

'Safety valve. Better than flash riots.'

'If you say so.'

'What do you know? You weren't in the force during The Emergency.' She was wasting her breath, but she couldn't help herself. 'Thousands were killed, including coppers.' *My father and Richard among them.*

'Yeah, well, I should've stayed in the army. Coppers are dying now, and what do we do? Bugger all.'

She glanced at him. He gripped the steering wheel, white-knuckled. A big man, yes, but he'd become bloated, his skin sallow and unshaven. Probably battling the liquid demon again. Recruited into the police force from the army after The Emergency, he'd remained under her command ever since. They'd fought the good war against crime, comrades-in-arms. Nights in surveillance together sharing greasy burgers and tepid coffee. Chasing down armed suspects, covering the other's back. Sessions in the pub after a bad day or a win. His divorce; her husband's death. Once, they'd known each other better than they knew their own families. But not anymore.

'How come you're slumming it with me anyway?' he said, his tone slightly less savage. 'Thought you were a desk general now. A politico.'

Tina sighed. 'Sick of politics.' She should be clearing her backlog of appraisal reports and preparing for this afternoon's meeting, but she longed for fresh air or what passed for it in central London.

'Yeah?'

'Yeah.'

'That's it? Not that you want some action?'

She ignored him and leaned forward to engage the drone monitor on the dashboard. She had one minute of in-car screen time before motion sickness would hit. A grainy picture appeared. A white square – the forensics tent. Ten or eleven police cars, and six vans. Was that an ambulance leaving? White suits and yellow jackets crawled around like ants, too many to count... Aah, the green face of nausea leered at her, and she tapped the screen off.

'See anything useful in that five seconds before you throw up your porridge oats?' said Luke with a sly grin.

'Scene's rammed. Parking this beast'll be a bitch. You scrape another ARV and bye-bye Luke's bonus.'

'Ouch.'

'The commander says your team's unruly.'

'Because I trashed a couple of squad cars?' A mangy looking dog ran out and he swerved. 'Shit. Missed.'

'No. We're talking complaints. From members of the public.'

'Troublemakers.'

'I've backed you but...'

'But?'

'Lay off the heavy-handed routine. I don't want a rep for police brutality.' He snorted.

'And go easy on Rana. Don't want to scare off a new DC.'

'She's like a fucking puppy, weeing in every corner. She needs house-training.'

'She's weeing in every corner, as you put it, because you're shouting at her all day.'

'She complained too?'

'No. But I'm not deaf.'

'So that's the real reason you're here is it?'

'What?'

'To keep me on a leash? Or because you don't trust me to bring this one in?'

Tina frowned. 'Don't be so thin-skinned.' She supposed he was defensive because of Tommy. Losing a fellow officer was like losing a brother, and their failure to find the killer had clearly unsettled him. It had unsettled all of them.

CHAPTER TWO

Brickfield Road Red Zone needed sturdier barricades, Tina thought. Although barbed wire spirals topped the steel palisades, there were gaps where the fencing panels met awkwardly, and these had been filled with what looked like chicken mesh. The bright red 'KEEP OUT' signs would do little to deter the determined; what's more, everyone knew that drone-cam surveillance regularly failed to deliver on its expensive promise.

Luke stopped the car at the checkpoint and slid down his window. A guard in army fatigues approached. Since the army had taken over manning the checkpoints, Red Zone security had become an uneasy coalition of police and army operations.

'Morning ma'am. Inspector. Been expecting you.' His head cam flashed at each of them and emitted a bleep, then another. 'All good. You guys've got quite a party going on down there.' He waved them through.

The overcast sky, bruised with purple, lay like a funeral shroud over the road ahead, and gave stark meaning to the phrase 'the death of the high street'. Steel grilles or boards fronted retail premises and buildings of indeterminate origin. Further on, teeth of broken glass bit into the yawning window spaces of disused industrial units. The old Beehive pub on the corner was burnt out, a carbon effigy of itself.

A uniformed PC directed them into a narrow turning, then marched on ahead and used elaborate hand signals to guide their vehicle into a tight space.

'Don't need your effing help, mate,' Luke mumbled.

A scruffy young lad, aged about ten, sat between the open back doors of a police van. His trousers were too short and his sweatshirt too big. A female officer perched beside him, her arm around his shoulders, holding him close.

'Looks like the finder,' Tina said.

'Yeah.'

'You see Mütter and Rana?'

'Right behind us.'

Tina was waiting for them as they pulled up. 'See what you two can get out of the finder. Log in first, clear it with the SOCO.'

Rana nodded. 'Got it, ma'am.'

Satisfied, Tina scanned the area. City East had been busy. The site hummed with uniformed police and white-suited forensics officers. The pathology tent and login desk were up and running. Inner and outer cordons secured the scene, although no one on this side of sanity would wander here. The plot stretched between the derelict Abbey Chocolate warehouse and Jimi's Car Renovations. Thirty or more old cars lay behind broken wire fencing, some blackened and burned. The properties' owners would be long gone, bankrupted by the decade's cascade of financial crashes. A reddish-brown bird hovered lazily above; a kestrel, perhaps.

It looked like a smear of dried blood against the dark sky.

'This'll be a bitch to search, what with all this junk.' Luke's voice broke in.

'Certainly will. What's down there?' She looked south. 'Beyond those shrubs?'

'More warehouses?'

'Don't think so. The canal, isn't it? Limehouse Cut?'

Luke shrugged.

'Might need to call in a dredging team,' she said.

'Oh joy.'

A white-suited figure waved, beckoning them.

'Let's go.' She headed towards the login desk, picking her way over the uneven ground. Weeds pushed their way through cracks in the concrete. A sapling had tried its luck but it was leafless, strangled by ivy.

She flipped out her warrant card. 'Detective Chief Superintendent Tina Andrews, Central Elite Police; this is DI Luke Sanderson.'

'Morning, ma'am. DI Sharon Watts, City East. Scene of Crime Officer. Hope you've had your breakfast.' She smiled, her lips tight.

'Mmm. Like that is it?'

'It's messy.'

Tina glanced at Luke, who hung back. 'You want a look? No? Not like you, Inspector. Too many beers last night?'

He wiped the back of his hand across his mouth and shook his head. 'Want me to co-ordinate the search? Before it pisses down?'

He had a point, she thought. Rain destroyed most forensic evidence. 'OK, yes. Fingertips to seventy-five metres both ways for starters. Have a scout down by the canal. Talk to checkpoint security and get a duty roster. And liaise with DI Watts here.'

DI Watts pointed to the metal plates laid on the ground which led to the forensics tent. 'Please stay on the common approach path when you go up, ma'am.' She shrugged apologetically. 'Got to say it.'

Tina made her way to the tent, stepping plate-to-plate. The rotund, white-suited shape of Felix Roberts stood just outside, stretching and rolling out his shoulders.

'Hello Dr Roberts.'

He pulled down his mask. 'Chief Superintendent. Congratulations on your promotion.'

'Thank you.'

'Strange times indeed when the Chief Super's the same age as my own daughter.' He fixed her with cynical eyes.

'Mmm.' She wasn't in the mood for Felix's existential despair and gestured towards the forensics tent. 'Moving on?'

'Whitish male, early twenties. Dismembered.'

'Anything on him? ID? Phone?'

'No.'

'DNA through yet?'

'Should be. I put a sample in the machine myself twenty minutes ago. Jones!' he called, turning towards the forensics van, 'What's come up on the RapidCode for DCS Andrews?'

Two white-clad figures were busy at a bank of machines inside the van's open doors. The smaller one looked up, shook her head and made a thumbs down gesture.

'There's your answer,' he said.

'Result's not through or he's not on the register?'

'Not on the register.'

'Bugger.'

'Happens. Last Public Control audit of the database showed only eighty-four percent population coverage, and that's a massaged figure in my opinion. Place is run by teenagers with the attention spans of fleas.'

'Last time we met you said eighty-nine percent,' Tina said.

'You want to debate population statistics *now*, detective?'

'You started it,' she said. She changed the subject. 'So doc, time—'

'Don't ask—'

'—of death?'

'You'll have to wait till I get him on the chopping board.'

She grinned. 'Ball park. A day? A week? A month?'

He sighed theatrically. 'Within the last twenty-four hours, I'd say. Rigor's gone, so more than twelve hours, probably not much longer. No sign of gnawing from rats or dogs. A few blowfly eggs in the wounds, but they can appear in minutes. And there's not enough blood.'

'Meaning?'

'Meaning, perhaps this isn't the primary scene. Or the damn rain's washed it clean. Or the amputations occurred postmortem. You want some gloves?'

She shook her head. She wasn't planning to touch.

'Well, come into my lair.' He held aside the door flap.

Tina stepped inside. Her eyes slid over the thing which lay on the ground, flat on its back. She felt disorientated and her breathing quickened. She knew the drill, counted her breaths in and out until she was sure of control.

Most bodies still looked like people, but this... this defenceless grotesquerie defied all reason. Her gaze slipped away. She found herself watching the photographer while he fiddled with his camera. Someone retched loudly outside the tent, to be yelled at by DI Watts for contaminating the scene. Dogs barked excitedly in the distance.

She tried again – got close, crouched down. There was an odd chemical smell. She'd expected the metallic odour of blood, the reek of urine or faeces.

'Can I smell fuel?' She glanced up at Felix.

He hunkered down beside her. 'An accelerant, yes. Look at his clothes. You can see it in those lighter patches, in the blood-soaked areas, with the darker lines around them: here, and here.'

'Doesn't look burned though.'

'No. Maybe the perpetrator got disturbed. Perhaps by the finders. Maybe he decided to burn the body; it started raining and he couldn't, or he changed his mind.'

'But the rain didn't wash the fuel off his clothes?'

'Some usually lingers. Accelerants and water don't mix.'

She nodded and turned her attention back to the body, forcing herself to look at the injuries. If you could call them injuries. The limbs were missing in surprising symmetry; both arms gone from just above the elbow; the legs taken from mid-thigh. The clean cuts had left stumps of dark, raw meat which were laced with strings of silver and spotted with black. Her throat burned at the sight of the exposed bone, and she swallowed hard. A woodlouse tracked a busy path across the brown-stained tatters of trousers that clung to his lower body. His jeans were now a parody of summer shorts — as if this limbless body could once have housed a carefree human spirit.

Tina had seen many bodies; occasionally bodies as mutilated as this. She always viewed the face last, because the face made the victim a human being. A person. Not a thing. And she couldn't look at the injuries after that. She held herself very still and finally studied his face, trying to picture the man that he had been. Young, not much older than her own son and daughter. His split, upper lip hung away and revealed two or three missing teeth. His nose was mashed. But there was something about him... the high cheekbones, the angle of his jaw... She leaned in closer, held her breath, and looked into his partly open eyes. Green, with a patch of amber in the left. Unusual. Had she seen this before somewhere? Come on Tina, focus. Focus. A breeze lifted a strand of his hair, and she felt a sudden impulse to stroke it. He was some poor woman's son. But the rising surge of pity was a useless sentiment, and she fought it.

Raised voices. She thanked Felix and stepped outside. The commotion involved Rana, Mütter and the finder kid. Rana, her fists clenched, glared at Mütter, who'd got the boy spreadeagled against a police van, and was patting him down. Tina hurried back along the common approach pathway as Mütter extracted something from the kid's pocket with a triumphant flourish. Fuck's sake, like she needed this. The man never used a light touch when a heavy one would do.

'—arresting you on suspicion of carrying an offensive weapon—'

Good God! Too late for Tina to intervene.

'Bullshit! You think I cut his legs off with this? You're insane!' The boy's voice finished on a high-pitched wobble. Bony ankles protruded from tattered jeans and his bare feet were crusted with black.

'You do not have to say anything but anything—'

'It's because I'm black! You said I done good—' He turned wounded eyes on Rana. 'You said I's right to call—'

'Shut it,' Mütter snapped. 'Anything you do say—'

'I w-want my mum.' He began to cry.

'Where is she?' Rana interjected.

'Gone!' he wailed. Snot dripped and landed on Mütter's shoe.

'Jesus. C'mon you.' He grabbed the kid's sleeve.

'Lemme go!' The boy squirmed and wriggled, then sank his teeth into Mütter's hand.

'You little sod.' He forced the boy's arms behind his back, cuffed him and bundled him towards a squad car, beckoning a PC as he went.

'Dick,' said Rana, not bothering to lower her voice.

'Cut it out,' said Tina. 'So. The kid?'

Rana's cheeks flamed crimson. 'Tyler. He and his mate, Jaden, bunked off school, came up here to hang out, the two of them. Anyways, they were smoking some shit, and Jaden saw something over there, see?' She pointed to the forensics tent.

'Go on.'

'They went to look. Tyler wanted to run but Jaden collapsed – he's got asthma. So Tyler helped him with his inhaler, phoned an ambulance. Paramedics called it in on their way. DI Watts says they've taken him to St Winifred's.'

'Rewind. Kid's got a phone?'

'Looks like a burner, ma'am. I bagged it.'

'Good. Got Tyler's address? Parents?'

'Gave me an address but it sounds fake. Think he sleeps rough, I mean, the state of him.'

'Mmm.'

Rana still bristled. 'Ma'am, he's only eleven, he could've just legged it. Don't suppose he even knew that carrying a flick was an offence—'

'Probably did know. Just forgot to dump it.'

'But all kids carry, ma'am, and Mütter just—'

'Enough. Go over to St Winifred's; see the other boy.'

Rana hesitated. 'Ma'am?'

'What?'

'There's something else.' She glanced sideways; dropped her voice.

'Well, spit it out.'

'Tyler was here last night.'

'After curfew?'

'Yeah, about nine thirty. I don't think Mütter heard that, I mean, he'll only charge him for breaking curfew as well, and—'

'I get it. Go on.'

'He was supposed to meet someone.'

'Who?'

'A "friend" he said. A dealer maybe, I guess he planned to score some dope, y'know—'

'And?'

'The friend didn't show but someone else did.'

Tina's pulse quickened. 'Did he give a description?'

'No ma'am,' she said bitterly. 'That's when Mütter came over playing bad cop.'

What a prick the man was. He resented Tina for all the predictable reasons – fast-tracked, too educated, too well-connected. Too young at thirty-eight to his fifty plus. She'd overheard him in the pub one night calling her 'an over-promoted bitch – shaggable, zilch else.' His interference today had jeopardised the success of the investigation.

Tina watched him direct a squad car out of the parking area. Tyler's woebegone face stared out of the rear passenger window.

'DS Mütter!' she called.

He pointed at his own chest in a pantomime version of 'Who, me?'

She nodded and crooked her index finger, beckoning him.

He walked towards her slowly. Tina began counting to ten. She got there, started again and reached seven, before Mütter had settled himself beside her, leaning back against the van, legs crossed at the ankle. He unwrapped a stick of gum and popped it into his mouth.

'What do you think you're doing?' she said.

A look of sly innocence slid across his face. 'The gum? Quitting smoking. You want some?' He proffered her the packet. Tina resisted the urge to drive her fist into his flabby gut, but it wasn't easy.

'The kid. The arrest. You shut down a potential witness mid-flow.'

'Zero tolerance for knife crime, Chief Superintendent, just following the rules.'

'Is that right, Sergeant Mütter? And do you know the rule that says you do not, repeat, do not, make an arrest at a crime scene without the say-so of your senior investigating officer?'

'Sorry ma'am. Assumed you were here as an observer. For reports and stuff. Thought Luke was the SIO, and I knew he'd be fine with it.' He smiled, a glint of yellow teeth.

She stepped up close until they almost touched and eyeballed him. Tina was five feet nine, plus a boot heel, and they were level. His breath smelled of mint with an undertow of decay. He tried to take a small step away, but he was backed against the van, and there was nowhere for him to go.

'Mmm. About reports and stuff. Your appraisal is on my desk. My office. Six o'clock.'

Mütter said nothing. The smirk had gone but his weasel eyes said, 'Bring it on.'

CHAPTER THREE

Tina left the crime scene at 1.20 pm and went directly to the Supreme Court in Westminster, prepping for the Appeals Process Committee in the back of a squad car. The meeting dragged. She presented the operational costs of policing the Pentonville People's riots, as they'd come to be known, in the previous April; riots that had seen the deaths of two police officers, and twenty-three members of the public. The longer that prisoners remained on death row in Pentonville, they all agreed, the greater the head of steam that fizzed amongst professional agitators in the community. The committee decided that the appeals process should be radically streamlined. Although Tina couldn't deny the logic of this, she had voted against it. The committee's decision rested uneasily upon her soul.

She exited the building at the back, into Little Sanctuary. A seagull landed hard on a fat pigeon in the cobbled road, shook it in its beak, and dropped it only to peck at the flesh. Nice. But where was her car? It was 3.35 pm – only twenty-five minutes until Tommy's funeral at Southwark Cathedral. She pulled out her phone. London Search displayed the Gov-jammer image – a smiley face with a wagging finger, the universal sign for denied access. She jabbed at the icon again. Smiley's pixelated face was still smirking.

'You see a police car come by?' she said, turning to the guard by the exit door. He looked like a statue, as if hewn from the grey stone that formed the façade, but his grip on the ArmaLite semi-automatic tightened visibly.

He shrugged.

She checked her messages. Eleven; three from Marcus. She tapped her PA's icon.

'Marcus? Where's my car?'

'Sorry, boss. Been and gone. Police Autos wouldn't wait for King William himself.'

'Is it coming back?'

'No. Driver was scared off by, and I quote, "a fucker with a fuckin' big-dick gun."'

'Shit.'

'I can send a driverless-electro? Westminster to Southwark... sixty-eight minutes. You wearing your trainers? You could run it in twenty,' he sniggered.

'Very funny, smart-arse. Next?'

'Underground's closed between—'

'It's always closed. Next.'

'Start walking south, down Little Sanctuary.'

She began to walk.

'There's a chopper at three forty-five, Westminster School heliport, five minutes. Four minutes for your long legs. Could take you to Potter's Field helipad, next door to the cathedral.'

'Thought Potter's Field was flooded?'

'Re-opened two weeks ago.'

'Mmm... better not.' Even Tina couldn't justify taking a helicopter to a funeral.

Marcus tutted. 'I promised sexual favours to young Millie to hold that chopper, and as you know I don't even swing that way.'

'Very grateful. So it's the river then?'

'It's the river but can I find an MPV, that's the sixty-four Euro-Billion question—'

'You've had your fun. When and where?' She was almost at the junction.

'Boat'll be at Westminster pier in six minutes. Cut through Parliament Square, cross the bridge, down to the river on your left, and Bobby Bingo.'

'Thanks.'

'Mine's a sweet vermouth and—'

She had already hung up.

Tina could smell the river before she could see it: rotten vegetation with the occasional waft of sewage. The tourists were long gone. Graffiti-scarred hoardings obscured the Houses of Parliament which had first flooded, then burned, when river water corroded the old electric cables and rendered them combustible. The long white drapes which cloaked the clock tower were now a dirty grey. Why had someone thought it a good idea to leave Big Ben's face exposed through a ragged hole in the cloth? Proud once, but now forlorn – like a defeated king who surveyed a ruined, ravaged land.

Armed security guards fronted the blockades which restricted access to the bridge. After Tina's ID had been scanned, she hurried across Bridge Street then down to Victoria Embankment where construction vehicles squealed alongside the river like angry, mechanical beasts seeking a place to cross. The Marine Police Vehicle waited at the pier, its chequerboard stripe surreally bright against the murky water.

A large, orange-jacketed officer watched her from the boat. 'DCS Andrews?'

'Yes.'

'DS Leroy Jameson, Marine Police.' He glanced briefly at her ID, and maintained eye contact a fraction longer than was necessary. 'Your taxi to Southwark awaits you, ma'am. Hop in.'

She 'hopped in'. The stink of sewage was bad here. She rummaged in her pocket for the tube of eucalyptus ointment that she carried everywhere, and smeared a little into each nostril, her eyes tearing up.

'Don't know how you stand it. The smell.'

He smiled, a flash of white teeth in a weather-beaten face. 'It's better in the middle of the river.' He handed her a life jacket. 'Come up front, I'll give you the tour.'

'OK.' She didn't need a tour but there was no point in being churlish.

'Want this?' He extended a headset. 'You can wire in your phone here.'

'Thanks.' She put it on and adjusted it.

He opened out the throttle. Tina turned her face into the cool wind which blew away the city dust as they picked up speed. She turned up her collar and tucked in her ponytail.

'Nice set of wheels,' she said into the microphone.

'Isn't she,' he said. 'Can do seventy-six knots at the top. Want a demo?'

'Not today,' she laughed. 'You do this job during the floods?'

'Yeah, was here for the big one three years back. Helped retrieve the bodies from the basement flats in Southwark. The flashy new developments in Pimlico got hammered too. Not complaining, keeps me in work. On a rolling contract though. They want to keep their options open in case they ever sort out that bleedin' glitch in the Thames Barrier. I blame the Chinese, myself.' He grinned at her. 'Reckon my job's safe for a few years yet. How about you, DCS Andrews? What's—'

Her phone rang. Marcus.

'Felix-up-his-own-arse-Roberts wants to know why you're not answering.'

'Huawei 12G?'

'That's what I told him. He wanted your InstaConnex code, so I said it was more than my job, no, more than my very sad little life was—'

'You can give him the code.'

'Diddly dandy. Love ya.' He rang off.

The New Scotland Yard building came into view on the left, and she couldn't help but look: it was like scratching a scab. Her father had been a section commander there. He'd taken her on a tour when she was fourteen; she'd pretended to be bored and flirted outrageously with his juniors, but secretly she'd been impressed.

Of course, it was no longer the New Scotland Yard building but the Mandarin Oriental NSY hotel, and the iconic, triangular revolving sign had been amended accordingly. Tina felt a stab of vengeful pleasure that the sign almost never rotated. The official line was water in the electrics, but she suspected sabotage by disgruntled police officers.

'Who stays in that place?' DS Jameson's voice crackled in her ear. 'The smell of shit, the sound of pneumatics, and dust in your mouth.'

'Rich people.'

'Suckers.'

'Mmm.'

The old Millennium Wheel loomed up fast on the right. It listed ten, maybe fifteen degrees over the river and DS Jameson steered the boat as close as possible beneath it – her driver was doing the river-boat equivalent of looping the loop. A wave of nausea washed over her.

He laughed. 'Don't worry chief, it's not gonna fall today.'

Her phone pinged – the InstaConnex message signal. Felix Roberts. She read:

Body part found, 15.25 h, 12.10.29
Thames foreshore Tower of London, 20 m west of Traitor's Gate
DNA match to victim CEBH-9174, Red Zone 13
Low tide, seventy minute recovery window

Tina's heart skipped. 'DS Jameson? Can we make a small detour via Tower Pier?'

'Sure thing, ma'am.'

The Tower was only a short hop from Southwark Cathedral. She could look in on the recovery site, then nip back for most of the funeral service. She turned her face into the sharp wind, and its cold slap made her skin tingle.

LUCY DIXON

Lucy Dixon is an editor, social media manager and podcaster. She lives in Suffolk with her seven-year-old son George, their dog and two cats. Alongside crime writing, she is also working on a non-fiction book about learning to walk again after contracting meningitis and spending five months in hospital.

Lucydixon79@gmail.com

Scars

CHAPTER ONE

Hackney, 2013

Nicky moved a small step closer to the bed, the only sound a slight squeak from her trainers. The only light a brilliant spot from the lamp at her side, directing its beam at the boy. His skin appeared pale blue, its smoothness marred by dark lesions. She focused her camera on his face. His skin was soft. Plump. But pitted with scars and, in places, angry red spots. Weeping. They covered his forehead and cheeks, with a scabby trail running under his chin and down his neck, spreading onto his chest. Erupting with pus. Nicky's finger pressed down on the camera's shutter button. It startled him.

'Just a few more and we'll be done, so please stay completely still.' The boy blinked his agreement. She preferred it when they didn't talk, although she'd become an expert at patient chit-chat over the years. Nicky pulled the lamp in closer to his face and gently raised his chin with her left hand, knowing she needed to document the extent of the scarring here. The shutter clicked, capturing the damaged skin, and also the boy's carefully controlled emotions. His shame. She hoped the treatment would work for him, that in a few months' time she would be taking new pictures to illustrate the progress made. That he'd be smiling again. But Nicky knew better than to say this. Hope was not always a good thing.

'Right,' she said, swinging the lamp around to illuminate the clipboard that was resting on the stool next to her. 'I have everything Dr Davis asked for now. You can get dressed and then you're free to go. We'll see you back in clinic in twelve weeks.' Nicky flicked on the room's light and smiled at the boy as he pulled on his T-shirt and jumper.

'Thanks very much,' he said, a slight blush appearing on his cheeks. Teenage boys were always so awkward, couldn't cope with interacting with adults. Especially women. He gave a slight wave, opened the door and disappeared down the corridor.

Nicky plugged the camera into her computer and sat down to start processing the shots she'd taken, glancing at the clock to check how long she had until her day's work finished. A cancellation meant the boy had been her last patient for the week. She opened up the photos with a few clicks of the mouse and waited while the hospital's computer system kicked into action. It was often a long wait, one she frequently spent daydreaming, staring at the hospital's logo spinning on her screen, her eyes occasionally refocusing to take in her reflection, her own undamaged skin, broken up with an increasing amount of wrinkles. Or what the advertising copywriters liked to call fine *lines*. Her phone vibrated on her desk. It was a text from Sally.

What time will you be back tonight? Can you pick up something for dinner? X

Nicky typed a quick response.

How's the revising going? I'll be home around 6. Do you want the usual from Benny's? xxx

She had just hit the send button when she heard the softest of taps on her door. It was Gavin. His afternoon break.

'Hey, are you free to talk for a minute?' he asked, sounding official. He pulled the door shut behind him and turned the lock with a loud clunk. The grin on his face suggested he didn't actually want to talk, of course, which was why Nicky liked him. He walked towards her, undoing the waist tie of his scrubs with one hand and reaching to spin her chair around with the other. Nicky was suddenly desperate to taste his skin. She reached for the blue cotton of his uniform and pulled him towards her, eager to lose herself in him.

This side of Nicky had only been back at the surface in the last year, once Sally started staying out sometimes, leaving her mum with space for acting irresponsibly for the first time in 16 years. She'd agonised over it for months, wondering whether she could risk seeking out some human contact. Worrying it would bring her carefully constructed sanctuary crashing down.

In the end, she had decided it would all work out as long as she avoided any man who wanted to talk. Any man who wanted to get to know her. Luckily, there were plenty of married men who wanted a passionate hook-up before they went home to their families. The internet was full of them. This hospital was probably full of them, too. The only words exchanged were usually filthy and there was no time – or need – for conversation. For a year she had enjoyed a series of one-night flings, some shudderingly awful and some shockingly good.

Until Gav, she had avoided anyone at work, preferring the anonymity and efficiency of the internet, and she couldn't shake off the worry that the loosening of her rules was a huge mistake. He had started working at St Giles about six months ago, as a nurse on the stroke ward, and their relationship, or whatever you would call it, started soon after. Nicky did sometimes wonder what it was about her that had given off the vibe she was the type who would be up for a quick fumble in the supplies cupboard, but she suspected it was a thread best left unpicked.

It had begun after the hospital's Christmas party. So utterly clichéd. She usually avoided any social events but had agreed to go in a moment of weakness and Gav had somehow sensed the need in her, lubricated by vinegary white wine in thin plastic beakers. After, she had been adamant it wouldn't happen again, that she wouldn't risk disrupting the job she loved for something so pointless. But a pattern of clandestine meetings had developed, and she seemed incapable of putting an end to things. Gav had an uncanny ability to know when his break times coincided with a gap between her patients, and he would turn up to the clinical photography office, instantly hard as he walked through the door. Initially he had tried to talk about his unhappy marriage, to make excuses for his behaviour.

'We've been together since school, we're more like brother and sister these days. We stay together for the kids. And it's easier financially,' he'd said that the very first night. Reeling off the script of cheating spouses the world over, before going on to lament the lack of sex.

'We all have needs, it's human,' Nicky had replied, knowing it was what he wanted her to say, but feeling embarrassed that they sounded like the problem pages of a discarded magazine in one of the hospital waiting rooms.

'That was so hot,' Gav sighed, untangling his fingers from Nicky's hair and pulling his scrubs up, before reaching for the antibacterial hand gel on her desk. She wordlessly watched him rubbing his hands together, pleased at the sight of his flushed cheeks. Her gaze moved to the large clock on her wall and she noticed just five minutes had passed. Five minutes of kissing and sucking, moaning and release. She reassured herself that nothing catastrophic could result from an act that took under five minutes. It was too insignificant to count. Gav leant forward and kissed her on the forehead.

'See you on Monday, you gorgeous woman.'

'Enjoy the rest of your shift,' she said with a smile, already switched off from him and wondering if Sally had replied about what she wanted from the deli.

'Sally! I'm home!' Nicky called out as she clattered through the front door, clutching a bottle of wine and a bag of food from Benny's. Using her hip to push the door shut behind her, Nicky kicked off her sandals and walked through the tiny hallway into the living room to see Sally sitting on the sofa with the dog, staring at the telly and fiddling with her strawberry blonde hair, loosely pinned back. She twirled it round her fingers as she'd done since she was a baby. Often it was a sign she was tired. Her charcoal skinny jeans were almost entirely covered by golden fur. Bella was definitely too big to be a lap dog, not that she seemed to realise this.

'Er, hello! I'm home! You've finished revising then? Are you hungry?'

'Sorry, Mum! Just let me pause—'

'Christ, you're not watching that tripe again, are you? Come and help me eat some of this. Benny went a bit over the top as usual.'

Sally switched off the telly and gently pushed Bella off her legs so she could join her mum in the kitchen, with the dog's paws clacking softly behind her across the stripped wood floor of the living room. In the kitchen, Nicky looked through the large window that looked out onto their back garden and then the park beyond. She saw their neighbour getting his washing off the line and pulled the roller blind down, its mint green fabric blocking the setting sun. Her hands delved into the bag of food. She pulled out foil trays of stuffed vine leaves and meatballs in garlicky sauce, a pile of thick, floury pitta and tubs of hummus. Half a dozen of Sally's favourites from the Greek deli that they went to at least once a week. Sally put two chipped plates and two mismatched wine glasses on the pine table, pulled out a rickety chair and sat down. Her pale blue gaze eagerly eyeing up the selection. Even after years of living down the road from Benny's, neither of them tired of the menu.

'How was your day?' Sally asked, scooping hummus onto her plate with a spoon and pouring wine into her glass with the other hand.

'Standard acne and boils, nothing out of the ordinary. Did you get much work done?'

'Yeah, I spent most of the day on biology, it's under control. Can't wait for these exams to be over so I can start enjoying the warmer weather. I feel like I haven't seen daylight for months and I swear I'm getting vitamin D deficiency.' Nicky suppressed an eye roll.

'It'll be worth it when you're qualified and spending every day cuddling kittens.'

'There's slightly more to it than that! Pass me the olives, will you?' Nicky handed her daughter the pot, a clove of garlic stuffed into each shiny olive.

'Did you get those photos done, Mum?'

'I take photos all day, Sal, you'll need to be more specific.'

'Mum! You know which photos I mean! The ones for your dating profile!'

'Oh, that. I'm still not sure it is a good idea, darling, I know you're trying to help but there are a lot of weirdos out there. I'm perfectly happy with you and Bella, why fix what ain't broke, or whatever that phrase is...'

'I'm not going to be here forever, Mum, and you promised you'd give it a go! Can't believe you are backtracking now. I've written your profile and it is all ready to go, once I have a photo. I could, of course, stick any old picture on but I wouldn't do that to you.'

'You've written a profile? Good God. What does it say? Read it to me.'

Sally picked up her phone and opened the note she had composed earlier.

'*Dog-loving 34-year-old woman looking for a man who doesn't mind holding the poo bags on beach walks. I usually prefer animals to people, but I am willing to be convinced by the right person that there is room in my heart for both. I love Greek food and swimming but always leave 45 minutes between the two.* That's the introduction bit, then I have added in all the details, you know, Nicky, auburn hair, photographer, the fact you have the world's best daughter, that kind of thing.'

'I don't know, it's kind of you to write this for me, but I don't think I'm ready.'

'For fuck's sake, Mum! You have never been on a date that I can remember and I am 17 years old! 17! When will you be ready? When you're 85? When *I* am?'

Nicky played for a bit of time before answering by clumsily knocking a slice of pitta on the floor. She smiled as she heard Bella's tail wagging in gratitude. With her daughter studying to become a veterinary nurse, she'd started monitoring what Bella ate and was becoming a bit of a moaner about it. One crisp for a dog was the equivalent of a human eating a whole multipack apparently. So, Bella had just hoovered up an entire loaf of bread in dog calories. Considering she was walked for at least five miles every single day, even when an icy wind was howling across the park and Nicky's face felt like it was being grit-blasted, Nicky couldn't see the harm in a few treats, but she was trying to be supportive of Sally's regime.

'I am not going to be distracted by you giving our dog type two diabetes. You said you would do this, and I'm not going to shut up about it. For me? Do you want me to worry about you while I'm at college? To fail my exams because I'm so worried about my poor, lonely mum? What harm could it do to try?'

Nicky sighed. She kept her face in a carefully considered expression of exasperation and mild annoyance. Inside, her heart was hammering against her chest and she could feel the panic rising from deep within her. The harm could be earth-shattering, but Sally didn't understand. She had no idea the lengths Nicky had gone to, to keep them isolated. Safe. How could she know? She clearly wasn't going to drop this though, so perhaps it was best to act at least as if she was willing to dip her toe in the water.

'OK, sweetheart, for you.'

CHAPTER TWO

Great Yarmouth, 1996

Nicky slipped her arm through Charlotte's and they walked, with purpose, along Lancaster Road and towards the seafront. Bare, white legs and chunky boots. A uniform of black dresses with denim jackets, indigo blue and the palest khaki. Straightened hair and black eyeliner. The weak sunshine had lost its heat as the day came to an end and Nicky shivered. The sea breeze whistled around the girls as they navigated an obstacle course of discarded chip wrappers and drink cans. A splash of ageing vomit. The lights from the amusement arcades flashed and the crash of the waves could just be heard over the beeps and bells of the games inside.

'Have you got any vodka left?'

'A mouthful or two.'

Charlotte passed her the plastic Panda Pops bottle from her jacket pocket and Nicky felt the warmth spread from her throat to her stomach as she took a large gulp. She hoped it would calm the butterflies. Even after five months of dating Jim, she was still nervous about the party. About meeting more of his friends. She knew they'd all be Jim's age, probably with jobs and cars and proper homes, and Nicky didn't want to seem immature. Jim had called her immature once, when they'd had a row about him eyeing that barmaid, and it had seemed like the worst insult in the world. To be a young, silly girl.

She was glad Charlotte was with her tonight; she made her feel better, that she was sophisticated enough to have a friend with their own place.

Charlotte was almost two years older. She looked after herself. She wasn't a giggler. She wasn't like the other girls Nicky knew from school, or even college. She was calm, but not in a shy way. She was a bit inexperienced when it came to drugs, but didn't act like a boisterous puppy on its first walk out of the house. She hoped her and Jim's mate Simon would get on. It wasn't meant to be a double date, but it would be convenient if they liked each other.

They walked towards The Pier pub and Nicky looked through the window. She could see Jim standing at the bar, Budweiser bottle in one hand and cigarette in the other. Simon stood next to him, concentrating as he made a roll-up, fag paper stuck to his lip as he teased the tobacco out of its packet. She felt her stomach do a little flip of excitement at the sight of Jim and the thought of the night ahead. She grinned at Charlotte as they walked into the packed bar, pushing her way through until she reached Jim and snaked her hand around his waist in welcome.

'Nick! You look beautiful! I'm so happy to see you,' Jim whispered in her ear, pulling her in for a kiss that left her feeling slightly breathless, before indicating to the barman that he wanted serving again. The bar was full of people trying to make eye contact with the harassed bar staff, but somehow Jim got their attention first and ordered four more beers, not bothering to ask if beer was what they wanted. He was good at commanding attention. Nicky would be surprised if he had ever felt the tiniest moment of doubt about anything. Jim expected to be served first, so he was.

'We'll have one drink in here then we'll head over to Harry's studio. He calls it a studio but it's more like a massive shed, he rents it to store his materials. It looks incredible with the lights going and the music pumping.' He handed them both a bottle, and one to Simon, who started talking to Charlotte as if they were old friends. He probably had no idea that he'd never met her before, since Simon was often too high to appreciate the finer details. Jim winked at Nicky, pulling her closer and cupping her left cheek with his hand. She breathed in the scent of him, couldn't get enough of the mix of smoke and beer and just him. Something spicy. He whispered in her ear, but she couldn't quite make it out. He kissed her and she felt his tongue slip into her mouth, realised he was giving her a pill. It tasted odd, a strange mix of sweet and bitter, and she quickly washed it down with beer.

'A little enhancement to get things going,' Jim said, his breath warm on her cheek. He held her hand and slipped another pill into her palm. It felt sticky and Nicky wanted to get rid of it before it disintegrated in her clammy hand. She tugged on Charlotte's arm and pointed towards the toilet.

Locked in the cubicle with Charlotte, her friend looked anxious.

'Look after me, won't you?' Charlotte whispered, both girls staring at the tablet on Nicky's outstretched hand.

'Of course I will, but you won't need me to, I promise.'

'How long does it take?'

'You'll start to feel something in half an hour or so. You'll want to dance. You'll love everyone. Make sure you drink plenty. Water, not just vodka.'

Charlotte put the pill in her mouth.

'I left my beer on the bar,' she said, and dry swallowed the pill, gagging slightly as the bitterness hit the back of her throat.

'What do you think of Simon?'

'He's OK, but he's not stopped talking about his mixing. I know more about his decks than I needed to. Are you trying to matchmake? Don't fuck off and leave me with him all night, will you?'

'Once he's had a few more drinks, he thinks he's on stage at the Hacienda. He's a right laugh though, heart is in the right place. Come on, let's get back in there and get off to this party.'

Back at the bar, Jim handed Nicky and Charlotte their beers then ran a hand through his hair. Nicky loved the colour of it, so dark it shone. She couldn't believe how beautiful he was. She sighed and leaned into him for another kiss, thinking she could feel the first tingling of the ecstasy spreading through her body. But maybe it was Jim's effect on her. She could feel Simon watching them.

'Put her down, Jim, the night is young! Drink up, ladies, and I'll order us a cab to Harry's place. We should arrive just in time for things to get interesting.'

CHAPTER THREE

Hackney, 2013

Sitting side by side on the patchwork sofa, Nicky and Sally stared at the laptop screen as Sally copied her mum's dating profile into the relevant boxes, while the photo she'd taken minutes before uploaded. A bowl of olives teetered on the arm of the sofa and Bella rested her head on Nicky's knee.

Nicky tried to ignore the swirling in her stomach, the acid rising to her throat making her feel like she could vomit at any moment. With each tap on the keyboard, was Sally letting the tiniest slivers of danger creep into their lives, ready to wrench everything apart at the seams? And what if Sally somehow stumbled upon the *other* site and her *other* profile? There were too many potential disasters in the mix and Nicky, as she did whenever she started to feel anxious, was running all the worst-case scenarios through her head on a terrifying loop. She took a large swallow of wine and tried to stop fidgeting. Sally would start to wonder if there was something more to all this panicking if she didn't rein it in a bit. It was one thing to have doubts and be nervous, but she was aware that her reaction might seem too strong and raise questions in her daughter's mind.

'We need to put a sentence or two here about what your ideal first date would be,' Sally said, pointing at the screen, thankfully oblivious to her mum's growing nausea.

'One that is cancelled,' Nicky laughed, a little too loudly.

'I'm writing *a sunny beer garden on a summer's afternoon*, that makes you sound relaxed and friendly. Normal,' Sally replied.

'With Daniel Craig?' Nicky's second attempt at humour was more successful and rewarded with a grin.

'Right, that's all finished. I'll just press 'save' and your profile will be live. Hand me your phone and I'll add the app for you, so you'll get notifications as the messages start flooding in.'

'I think it'll be a trickle rather than a flood, if anything at all.' Meaningless sex with strangers was easy to come by, but Nicky suspected decent men you'd actually want to talk to would be thin on the ground.

'OK, well then let's have a look at some of the men's profiles, nothing wrong with being proactive. It is 2013 after all!' And before Nicky could object, Sally had typed in a few search terms and a screen of men's faces had appeared.

'I've put up to age 45, you don't really want any older than that,' Sally explained, as she scrolled down the page, moving the screen too fast for Nicky to take much in.

'This one looks nice, Mum, his name is Chris and he works in retail management. He has two children, younger than me but that's understandable, lives in Bow. Ideal first date is a pub lunch and then bowling. Oh. No. Cancel that.'

'What? What's wrong with him?'

'His other photo is just a picture of his car, and everyone knows that's a red flag for being a complete wanker.'

Nicky sipped her wine silently while Sally gave a running commentary of the profiles she was looking at, wondering when her daughter became such an expert in online dating. Her own profile had been live for fifteen minutes now and the ceiling hadn't come crashing down, so she felt slightly calmer. Maybe she had been getting worked up for no reason. When she thought about it rationally, which was hard to do, it did seem unlikely that Jim had spent the last 17 years trying to find her. And even if he had, the chances that he was trawling through the hundreds of dating sites and apps there were these days, and would somehow happen upon her profile, seemed incredibly slim.

'How about this one, Mum? He's a logistics manager, whatever that means, has been single for four years. Not quite as long as you but then nobody has been single as long—'

'I have been rather busy looking after you—'

'I know, I know! But you don't need to keep sacrificing yourself for me anymore. I don't need looking after. I haven't needed it for a while. Wouldn't it be nice to meet someone who could...' She waved her hand at the laptop. '...Go walking in the Lake District or wine tasting in the South of France?'

'Maybe you should leave me to have a look through these in peace and go and get an early night. You have a shift in the morning, don't you?'

Sally nodded, smiling in a rather smug way that suggested she thought she had won the debate, and gave her mum a kiss on the cheek. With Bella ambling behind, she went upstairs to get ready for bed. Nicky had noticed that just lately this involved a pretty complicated skincare routine that, she was assured, would get rid of all the 'toxins'. Quite what Sally thought her skin had picked up after a day at home revising, Nicky wasn't sure, but she was grateful every day at her daughter's responsible approach to every aspect of her life, so didn't want to comment. She could hear the ancient boiler kicking in as Sally presumably filled the sink with warm water and bubbles, under the always admiring eyes of Bella.

Nicky stared at the laptop as if she was waiting for it to explode. She knew how easy it was to find someone online, she'd been checking up on Jim since the internet was invented and her search skills were pretty damn good, as a result. She often searched for herself too, to make sure she wasn't traceable. The thought that her photo was now on a dating site for anyone to see made her throat feel suddenly restricted, as if she couldn't quite get enough air. Anyone could be running their eyes over her picture, reading Sally's words, and she had no way of knowing who they were.

Should she delete the profile and hope that Sally forgot about it? No, that obviously wouldn't work. Her daughter had been banging this particular drum for the best part of six months and was hardly likely to move on so easily. Maybe she could swap her photo for someone else's and assume that Sally wouldn't check. As the different possibilities fired around in her brain, Nicky looked around at the home she had built for her and Sally, a place that had felt like their own secret den for so long and wondered if it still needed guarding quite so enthusiastically. The last four times she had looked for Jim, since he'd been out, he'd been in Sunderland living with his sister. He was almost 300 miles away and had absolutely no idea where Nicky was.

Maybe he didn't care.

MARK HANKIN

Mark Hankin has published five crime thrillers under the pen name Timothy Frost. *Who Touches Me Is Broken* is written under his own name. He lives with his wife in North Norfolk.

www.timothyfrost.com
mark_hankin@hotmail.com

Who Touches Me Is Broken

PREFACE

My first contact with Ken Sinclair came on Thursday 14th March 2019 in a private message from a Facebook group called 'Writers Helping Writers':

Dear Mark
My name is Kenneth Sinclair (Ken). I have written my memoirs, focusing on an extraordinary period in my life during October 1988. I was then a graduate trainee reporter aged 21 on the *Today* newspaper. The editor sent me and my colleague Sarah, another trainee who had become my girlfriend, to the Clyde Submarine Base, where the British nuclear deterrent (then Polaris) was stationed. Working undercover, we were drawn into events so bizarre and momentous that even today I can scarcely believe they happened. But they did, and I have the records and documents to prove it, including a handwritten letter given to me by Margaret Thatcher at 5.08am on Thursday 13th October 1988 in her suite at the Grand Hotel, Brighton.

I am a journalist by trade, not a novelist, and I need some help to finish and polish my book. At present it reads rather like Ben Macintyre. Nothing wrong with that, I like his true spy stuff, but my story is more personal than historical.

In short, Mark, my manuscript needs 'sexing up' – quite literally, in a number of places!

I noticed from your posts that you offer ghostwriting services. I checked out your own books written under your pen name Timothy Frost, and realised you could be exactly the person to help me. I have read all five of your novels. The ones I particularly enjoyed were your comedy-thriller *The Abigail Affair* and your dark story of professional musicians and financial corruption *Play the Piper*. With all your books, once I started I couldn't put them down, and read every minute I could, actually wearing out the page turn button on my trusty old Kindle halfway through *Fight for Life!*

Forgive me, but it also helps that you, like me, are of an age and generation to remember the 1980s and the way things were then: technology, politics, cars, music, dress, girls, hairstyles etc.

If you are interested, let's meet up soon to discuss my project. I cannot offer you a fee for your work, but I have an alternative proposition you may find attractive. Unfortunately, my health prevents me from travelling, so will you be able to come and visit me in Nottinghamshire?

I look forward to hearing from you.

Ken Sinclair

I reread the message several times, alarm bells jangling. I was busy editing the final draft of a book of my own for publication, and had no wish to use up a day of my time and a tank of fuel on an amateur, a fantasist or (sad possibility) someone with dementia.

I didn't like the sound of his 'alternative proposition'. I'm a full-time professional author, and my ghostwriting (some of it for big names – you'd be amazed!) is all paid for at top market rates. Ken's praise for my fiction was a predictable ploy, and I wondered if he had done more than flick through the free Kindle samples of my books. The implausible mention of Margaret Thatcher, with its pedantic time reference, also worried me.

Wary but intrigued, I Googled 'Ken Kenneth Sinclair reporter journalist Today newspaper 1980s'. No hits that included *Today,* but that was hardly surprising given the title folded in 1995. I did get results from various magazines including *Shooting Times* and *Bike,* but couldn't be sure if these were the same Ken Sinclair. If so, his areas of expertise were... obviously... guns and motorcycles. Another warning flag.

I dithered for twenty-four hours, then sent a polite message declining his invitation.

I believed that would be the end of the matter.

I was wrong.

A few days later I received another message from Ken. This one included a single-paragraph synopsis of his memoirs (what the publishing industry calls an 'elevator pitch'). He also offered to email me a list of typographical errors in my own books that he 'thought I'd want to fix', and finished up with:

I should have been more clear about my financial proposition. Whilst I cannot pay you a guaranteed fee, I can offer a generous royalty-sharing agreement. Please reconsider. I don't want to go on to my second choice of collaborator.

I didn't respond, but later that day he sent over his list of errors anyway: a Kindle clippings file of thirty-seven typos, spread across all my books. If nothing else, this proved he had read all my output, and with extraordinary attention to detail.

I emailed Ken's messages plus my own thoughts and reservations to my long-suffering agent Sophie Silverman. She phoned me back fifteen minutes later in high excitement, saying it was the most intriguing pitch she'd seen for years, whether true or not it smelled like a bestseller, why was I so cynical and distrustful, what did I stand to lose apart from a day's editing, and I needed to get out more anyway.

(Sophie is relentlessly positive and upbeat, and bosses me as if I were half her age instead of the other way round.)

Despite serious misgivings, I emailed Ken back agreeing to visit him.

He hadn't been exaggerating when he said his health was poor: the home address he gave for our meeting was a hospice.

I arrived shortly before midday on the following Tuesday. Banks of daffodils provided a guard of honour as I drove up to the car park of the modern low-rise complex. I signed in and sanitised my hands as instructed. A care assistant took me to Ken's room. 'He's very weak,' she said before ringing his doorbell. 'No close contact, please.' She offered me coffee which I accepted.

Ken Sinclair lay in bed, connected up to drips and drains and oxygen: a small man, doubtless further shrunken by his illness. Incongruously, his hair was thick, dark and curly. Then I realised it must be a wig.

He greeted me with a wan smile and a wave of his free hand. Grey-skinned, gaunt and frail, he was clearly not long for this world.

I took the visitor's chair.

'Welcome, Mark. Ken Sinclair. Sorry, I mustn't shake hands. I am living – no, dying – proof that forty-plus a day is an unwise habit.' He spoke softly and with effort. 'The draft manuscript is on the table by the window. The brown suitcase contains my notes and documents. Have a read and a rummage and tell me if you can help. Take all the time you need. I'm not going anywhere. I may doze off.'

I crossed to the bay window which overlooked the gardens. The care assistant brought in my coffee and I set to work.

I began with the manuscript and spent an hour and a half skim-reading and making notes. Then I explored the elderly leather suitcase on the floor. This contained reporters' notebooks; Snappy Snaps wallets stuffed with six-by-four inch photo prints; a scrapbook of newspaper cuttings from *Today*, some with Ken's by-line, dated August to October 1988; cuttings from national newspapers, most dated 11th October 1988; a photocard Press pass to the 1988 Conservative Party Conference showing a very young bespectacled Ken; more cuttings, loose, mostly from the 1990s, from assorted rifle, car and motorbike magazines; a box of Dictaphone tapes plus the original handheld dictating machine; two CVs, one typed on a manual typewriter and the other printed on a dot matrix printer (the type that screeched like a miniature circular saw); a tiny vintage Pentax camera; recent PDF printouts of 1980s Cabinet papers downloaded from the National Archives; more official papers and typewritten reports, many stamped 'TOP SECRET', which looked like old photocopies; long curling faxes, faded to near-illegibility; a 1988 woman's pink Filofax; homespun Roneo-ed newsletters on coloured paper entitled *Faslane Focus*; the handwritten letter from Margaret Thatcher, prime minister in 1988, and another even more extraordinary document also in her hand on three sheets of A4.

I examined the Thatcher papers closely, even held them to my nostrils and inhaled.

Like everything in the suitcase, they were either the most elaborate, expensive, artful, accomplished, professional forgeries.

Or genuine.

I stood, stretched and returned to the bedside chair. Ken opened his eyes.

I said, 'May I record our discussion, please, to save taking notes?'

'Good plan. I used my Dictaphone all the time back in the day.'

I set my iPhone on the arm of the chair. 'I'll take it on,' I said.

'Good. Can you make it read like a novel?'

'Yes. It is already extremely well written, and could be published just as it is. But I think I understand what you are after. This is more than a memoir. It's actually a four-hundred-page love letter, isn't it?'

He thought about this for a moment. 'Yes. I suppose it is.'

I continued, 'We need more dialogue and more scenes. You have written mostly in narrative summary, with little direct speech. The facts and the events are all there, but without the emotional heft that a first-person account can give. And we must provide a physical setting for every chapter.

At present there's too much soliloquy and exposition floating around in a narrative ether. I recommend we anchor everything to the time and place.'

'Yes again.'

'Also, you write from the viewpoint of an older man looking back. It would read better if the voice was yours as a young man. So, no retrospective self-judgement, no giving away what's coming up, and cut out phrases such as...' I consulted my notes... '"Thirty-five years of frustration with mobile communications began that morning when I saw a light labelled NSVC glowing". That takes us out of the moment. The young you didn't know that mobile signals would still be so hopeless today.'

'Yes, yes, of course. I get all that. Still, the older Ken is the one telling the story. Could we have a section from the present-day me, perhaps to introduce Chapter One? Like a voiceover at the beginning of a film? Then step back to 1988.'

'A framing of the narrative? That's a traditional device and would work very well.'

'What about the footnotes? Do they add or distract?'

'I love them. They're a great way to explain stuff without holding up the story. Let's put in an Index and Glossary too. Britain in the eighties is a far-off land for anyone aged under fifty.'

A moment's silence followed. I lowered my voice and said, 'How much of it is true, Ken?'

'Every word. I'm a journalist. I report things. I don't make them up. Can't. I verified everything and cross-referenced it to the source material. Even the time checks and temperature readings are accurate. You'll find them in my notebooks. I was a right nerd. Still am.'

I said, 'It would be good to reproduce some of your documents in the book. The two CVs, for example. They're so sweet. And the official version of the events, which seems to differ in places from your first-hand account.'

Ken grew more animated than I had seen him. 'Yes, yes! We'll do that. Give the reader both sides.'

'And a selection of your photos. The portrait of the two of you in your undercover disguises, for example.'

He chuckled softly. 'I believe I may have invented the "selfie". I constructed a gadget using an aluminium window stay, a tripod fitting and a remote shutter release. It worked a treat on the Pentax with the 18mm lens fitted. I tried to interest Jessops in manufacturing it, but they thought the market would be tiny for something so specialised.'

I said, 'You realise this book is dynamite, even after so many years?'

'I do. We'll need a lawyer to vet the manuscript. We must get it cleared by MI5 and the Ministry of Defence too. I don't want you prosecuted under the Official Secrets Act.'

'Would you like me to rewrite a sample chapter, to show how I would tackle it?'

'Yes. Very much. How about the one before the incursion, where Debbie comes for Sarah and catches the two of us *in flagrante delicto*?'

'I imagine that was very funny.'

'Indeed it was.' He chuckled again, and his laughter morphed into a rasping rattle of a cough. A minute or more elapsed before he was able to catch his breath, reach out a shaky hand for a sip of water and continue. 'A USB thumb drive with the Word file is in my bedside drawer. Take it, and the suitcase.'

'There are many loose ends,' I said. 'Apart from the obvious unanswered question.'

'That's all for the Epilogue, which I have been unable to write. I can't manage my MacBook any more prone like this for long, and most of the time I'm too woozy from the morphine. May I brief you now, Mark? They say I have days or weeks rather than months.' He spoke without fear or self-pity.

'Of course.'

I realised I'd accepted the assignment without talking about money. I'd be in trouble with Sophie. I said, 'We do need to discuss my remuneration. You mentioned royalty share.'

'A fifty-fifty split, with my half going to nominated charities and voluntary organisations. That should give you a good return and a strong incentive to do your best work. And the donations will serve as my atonement.'

'Very generous. I'll have to run it by my agent, but I can't see a problem.'

'I'll get my solicitor to draw up an agreement. She's coming in later with some changes to my will.'

I started on my list of questions. After thirty minutes I had most of the answers I needed, but Ken had visibly tired. The arrival of the nurse to tend to his pain relief was my cue to depart.

I drove home in afternoon sunshine, Ken's suitcase in the boot and his USB drive in my pocket, wondering if my new client would survive even long enough to read my sample rewrite.

Mark Hankin
The Creakes, North Norfolk, November 2019

XIII

When I was one-and-twenty
I heard a wise man say,
'Give crowns and pounds and guineas
But not your heart away;
Give pearls away and rubies
But keep your fancy free.'
But I was one-and-twenty
No use to talk to me.

When I was one-and-twenty
I heard him say again,
'The heart out of the bosom
Was never given in vain;
'Tis paid with sighs a plenty
And sold for endless rue.'
And I am two-and-twenty
And oh, 'tis true, 'tis true.

From *A Shropshire Lad* by A E Housman (1859–1936)

CHAPTER ONE – ARRIVAL

My name is Ken Sinclair and this is my true story.

I know where it ends, but it's a little harder deciding where to begin.

If I were a movie director, shooting the film of the book, I would open with a drone shot from on high. An elderly Volkswagen camper van winds along the side of a Scottish loch on a dreary autumn day, to the soundtrack of *Never Gonna Give You Up* by Rick Astley. A caption appears on screen: 'Wednesday 5th October 1988, 1.35pm, 12°C, steady drizzle'.

Cut to exterior close-up through the windscreen. The wipers labour back and forth, clearing two interlocking semicircular areas of glass which frame the young occupants.

He is driving. His hair is longer than is fashionable for the era. Despite the weather, he wears sunglass clip-ons over his spectacles.

She also has big hair, a candy floss mass that's been Afro-ed, backcombed and spiked, then the ends dyed blonde, the whole effect that of a starburst on firework night. Or a small, adorable nuclear explosion. She wears heavy black eyeliner and mascara underneath chiselled Gothic eyebrows, like Siouxsie from the Banshees.

He and she have been lovers for fifty-four days.

She will be missing, presumed dead, by the end of the story.

Neither of them can guess at this as they approach their destination, singing alternate lines of the cheesy Rick Astley song.

The camper van indicates, slows and draws up outside the gates of a ramshackle caravan site by the roadside. He turns off the cassette player. She reaches into the glovebox and takes out a pink felt drawstring bag.

Let's start here.

CHAPTER TWO – PEACE

Wednesday 5th October 1988, 1.38pm, 12°C, rain

I pulled the camper van off the road, through the gates and on to a bumpy forecourt of mud and sodden cinders.

All seemed quiet, with no peace protesters in evidence. The steady Scottish drizzle must have sent them to ground.

I applied the handbrake and cut the engine.

I recorded the time and temperature in my notebook, fresh from the stationery store and marked 'KS1' with a Dymo vinyl label maker.

I turned to Sarah and snorted with laughter.

'What's the joke, Maverick?' she said.

'I still can't believe you did that to your hair. And now we have the earrings.'

'Just following instructions. Blend in.' She stuck out her tongue. 'You look equally ludicrous in those shades.'

I said, 'Definitely a Kodak moment.' I reached for my Pentax, screwed on the self-portrait device and we leaned together in our karaoke duet pose.

Only then did I unclip my oversized *Top Gun* aviators, at which point the scene outside acquired some muted colour.

My first impression was of a South African township, with wooden shacks, caravans, tarpaulins stretched between trees, rusty oil cans serving as rubbish bins or braziers and massive cable reels on their sides as makeshift tables.

A sign on painted corrugated metal sheets announced 'FASLANE PEACE CAMP' against a rainbow adorned with multiple CND symbols. Below this, a cartoon missile emerged from a submarine afloat in a loch. Hands of all colours reached out, and Munch-like faces silently screamed, 'NO CRUISE! NO TRIDENT!'

A hand-painted sign on a shack read, 'INFORMATION – LEGAL SUPPORT – VISITORS WELCOME'. The door stood open, and smoke puffed in a homely fashion from a flue jutting through the tin roof.

'Guess we check in there.'

We'd made it from London in two days, taking turns to drive, Sarah's Bon Jovi/Rick Astley compilation at maximum volume. We stopped for the night in a layby between Carlisle and Gretna Green, where we heated a can of baked beans with frankfurters, brewed tea and smoked a joint before retiring to give the VW's suspension a good workout.

We'd bought the camper from a Crocodile Dundee impersonator in the Caledonian Road for £350 in petty cash doled out by the editor himself. I was falling in love with the old van, its hooded chrome headlights so like the eyelids of a forlorn but faithful hound, and I was already in love with Sarah.

'Are you going to sit there daydreaming?' Sarah's voice cut through my reverie. I wound down the driver's window of the VW. This was necessary in order to get out, as the inside door handle was missing.

Before I could open the door a tall guy around six foot with an aquiline nose and short hair, wearing a full-length transparent plastic mac, ambled out of the reception shack.

He peered in through my window. 'Hey. Welcome to Faslane. Just visiting or do you plan to stay? I'm Jerry. Camp Commandant.' American accent, toothy grin.

'Ken,' I said, 'and this is my girlfriend Sarah. We'd like to stay a week or so, if you'll have us. Keen to join the struggle.'

Jerry stared across me at Sarah. 'That's quite a hairdo. You two come far?'

'London.'

'You'll have visited Greenham Common on the way, then.'

Sarah said, 'No' at the exact instant I said, 'Yes.'

'Make your minds up, guys!'

I laughed. 'Yes, we passed it. No, we didn't stop there.'

'It's a women-only camp,' Sarah explained. 'No one with a penis allowed in. We couldn't both stay.'

'OK. Rules for this camp: no alcohol, no drugs, no loud music after ten at night, no direct action without a resolution at Camp Fire, help with the chores, love everybody. There's no hierarchy and I'm not a commandant or leader or anything. You cool with that?'

We chorused, 'Yes,' and Sarah nodded, jangling her oversized earrings.

'Back up over by the gate. Tuck yourself in. You'll be fine there provided you can sleep through the all-night construction traffic.'

'Will do. Thanks, man.'

Jerry leaned in further and dropped his voice. 'One more thing.'

'Yes?'

'Tone down the act a bit. You two are straight out of Central Casting.' He turned and sloped off back to his lair.

I wound up the window, started the engine and manoeuvred the van into the corner site.

Sarah said, 'Looks like he rumbled us, Maverick.'

'Guess it's because we're clean and don't have BO.'

'We can soon put that right. I suppose we do look pink and scrubbed. We should have shopped at Oxfam. Our clothes are too new. Damn.'

'You were quick with that line about men not welcome at Greenham Common.'

'I'm Oscar material, you know that.'

'Almost like Jerry was expecting us,' I mused.

We got out. Opposite us stood a lopsided psychedelic caravan with a sign saying 'MAKE BAIRNS NOT BOMBS. APPLY WITHIN FOR DETAILS'.

Sarah said, 'At least it's stopped raining. Hello, who's this?'

'This' was a small boy running up, dressed in an orange one-piece nylon jumpsuit and pink wellies.

'I'm Archie. I'm four nearly five. You're pretty,' he informed Sarah.

'Well thank you, Archie, what a nice thing to say. I'm Sarah and this is Ken. What's that you've got?'

Archie held up a Fairy Liquid-bottle submarine with a cotton-reel conning tower and pencils for missiles. 'We're here because we don't want this to happen. Watch.' He crouched down, then jumped up and threw his model in the air. 'Psshwhoo!'

He retrieved his homemade Polaris and reinstalled the missiles with patient, chubby fingers.

'Did you make that all by yourself?'

'Yes. Joan helped. The toilet is there.' Archie pointed. 'The lock doesn't work so you close the door if you're a lady or you're doing a poo, that means keep out.'

The door of the toilet caravan opened. A girl stepped down and approached us. 'Hi guys. Welcome. I'm Debbie.' Younger than us, taller than both of us, blonde hair tied back.

'Ken and Sarah.' I extended my hand (hoping she had been able to wash hers) but Debbie marched straight up to Sarah and enveloped her in a hug. Then I received the same treatment. Debbie smelled of salt and soap. A tattoo of intertwined doves on her shoulder peeked out from under her home-knitted jumper.

'Peace, Ken.'

'Yeah, peace.'

'Come on, Archie, Colin and Joan will be back soon.' She took the boy's hand, turned to us. 'Archie's mum and dad. They've gone to town to sign on. You two on the dole or have you got dosh?'

Sarah said, 'We have some savings but we need to sign on too.'

'Helensburgh Job Centre. The bus stops right outside. I love your earrings, sister. You both members? Which branch?'

Once again Sarah had the answer. 'I bought these at university last year. We haven't joined yet.'

'The peace camps are separate from the Campaign for Nuclear Disarmament. We believe in peace everywhere – Palestine, Burma, South Africa. We want Nelson Mandela released. CND is fine, lots of people belong, but they do try and dictate to us. They're not so keen on direct action – they only care about numbers at the big demos. You guys got any hash?'

At last, a question I could answer. 'Yes. But Jerry said no drugs or alcohol.'

'Not at Camp Fire, or when public are around, or outside where the police could see you. In your van is fine, same with booze. Sarah, I need more members for the Sisters' Swimming Club. You game, girl? Start the day right. Might muss your stellar hair and make-up though.'

'Sure,' Sarah said. 'How many go?'

Debbie stood for a moment admiring Sarah. She reached out and fondled one of her jangly six-inch rainbow-coloured enamel CND earrings. 'Bev comes when she's around. Usually it's just me. I'll give you a knock at seven-thirty.' She indicated the VW camper. 'Nice rig. Archie, let's go, man.'

CHAPTER THREE – LOVE

Evening of the same day, 6.05pm, 9°C

'If not us, who?' Jerry called out.

'Us!' we chorused.

'If not here, where?'

'Here!'

'If not now, when?'

'Now!'

It reminded me of the 'Dib Dib, Dob Dob' of my Wolf Cub pack, but it seemed to energise the peace campaigners on this damp and gloomy Scottish evening.

We sat in a semicircle on logs, milk crates, salvaged car seats and camping chairs, hands linked as for *Auld Lang Syne*. That was no problem with Sarah next to me on the right, but on my left sat Jerry, and holding hands with him spooked me out. How hard should you grip? Would we have to sit like this for the whole evening?

The fire in the centre of the group provided a flickering illumination, accented by the glow of cigarettes. The smoke proved little deterrent to the notorious Scottish midges, which prompted frequent slapping and waving of hands around the circle.

We had agreed that I would observe the men, Sarah the women. Good practice for a reporter: remember names, faces and key facts without recourse to notebook and Sir Isaac Pitman's ingenious system.

One by one, the campers identified themselves and declared their dedication to the cause. Some stood, others leaned forward earnestly.

'Colin. Resident since 1986 with Joan and our beautiful son Archie.' (Said son lay asleep in his mother's arms.) 'Five arrests, two nights in jail.'

Joan said, 'Peace to all. One love, one life, one world.'

Both seemed about our age. Scottish accents, but not Glaswegian. Possibly from Edinburgh? I had no idea, really.

Next up, a huge hairy Yeti with Elvis sideburns. 'Mitch. Weegie, in case you didnae guess. I'm a sparkie, worked with some of the lads on the Trident site. Bluudy hair-raisin' stories they tell. Here for a wee spell to install them solar panels from Greenpeace. Should have some leckie tomorra.'

'Debbie. Six arrests, four nights in jail. Part-time hellraiser. Full-time gentle angry woman in a world of mad men. Making a difference, one day at a time.'

Next up, a skinny punk teen with a foot-high fluorescent green Mohican, studs in his nose and rings in his ears.

'Tony. General troublemaker and piss-taker.'

Tony couldn't be older than seventeen.

My neighbour released my hand and stood.

'Jerry. A friend from over the water. I've been active in the US anti-nuclear movement for years. I spent time at the Nevada test site. Got arrested along with Martin Sheen and Kris Kristofferson. Came over last fall for a conference, resident here for nine months. I'm a lawyer, so bring me your questions about NVDA[1]. I'm not licensed to practise here, so don't ask me to represent you if you're arrested. And yes, I do have a valid visa.'

Jerry sat. I kept my hands firmly clasped and in my lap. He turned to the man on his left, a scrawny individual with tattoos on his neck and hands and probably many other parts of his anatomy.

'Norman. Ex-Royal Navy rating on the Polaris bombers. I drop in here every few weeks, tell a story. I'm a chef in civvy street now.'

'No jam tarts tonight, Norm?' Colin asked.

'Nah, sorry, mate. Can't sneak a tray out every time.'

Jerry said, 'Now please welcome and give a sign of peace or love to our brand new arrivals, up from London in their smart VW camper van.'

I rose to my feet. Pins and needles shot through my calves from perching on a log. A heavy vehicle passed on the road and I waited until I could be heard.

'Thanks, Jerry and everyone, for such a warm welcome on a chilly evening.'

'Call this chilly? This is bloody tropical, mate. Wait till you're standing in a puddle outside the base for four hours holding a banner with rain running down your arms.'

'Don't mind Colin. Carry on, Ken.'

'I'm Ken and this is my girlfriend Sarah—'

Now Debbie piped up. 'With respect, Ken, women aren't chattels. We don't own each other and she can speak for herself. Tell us about *you*, man!'

I began to feel the panic of a wannabe stand-up taking flak on open mic night.

'Sorry, Debbie, I'm just so proud and humble to be in a relationship with this wonderful woman. I'm a photographer, at least I plan to be. Got this baby for a twenty-first birthday present.' I held up the miniature Pentax. 'Lots of my mates went into advertising or commercial graphics. I'm more

---

[1] Non-Violent Direct Action.

into photography in the service of activism: Jeff Wall, the Düsseldorf school, if you're familiar with them.' I looked around the circle of faces in the flickering firelight, and sensed that my fellow campers were in no way familiar with the Düsseldorf school or possibly any contemporary art movement. 'With your permission, I'd like to make a photographic record of the peace camp in action. Get powerful images of resistance, like Leon and Jill Uris did with their book about the Troubles.' That produced some nods of approval at last. 'Or Don McCullin, with his pictures from the front line. Is everyone cool with me snapping them here day to day, and on the protests?'

I waited a beat. No one voiced an objection. Jerry said, 'We often have journalists turn up here, they're very welcome, but they have their own agenda, obviously not the same as ours. So yeah. Perfect, Ken. Just take care if you shoot near the base. The cops will try and confiscate your gear.'

I breathed out. I'd got away with my tissue of lies.

HELEN JONES

Helen Jones is a crime fiction MA student and former journalist, translator and marketing director. She was shortlisted for the Writers' Retreat short story competition in 2019. Helen lives in a village on the North Downs in Kent, with her three teenage children and a cat called Rodney.

helenjonesie@gmail.com

Broken English
An extract from the midpoint of the novel

Piers was waiting for Erin with a look of thunder on his face. 'Where the fuck have you been?' he said.

'Andreou needed to speak to me.'

Erin pushed past him and walked through the front door, but he caught her arm and pulled her back. 'Been to the police without me again? If I didn't know better, I'd think that you were trying to hide something from me.'

'I've got nothing to hide from you.'

'Sure about that?' Piers's face was red, his breathing erratic.

Erin nodded.

'Who was at the police station with you?'

'Police Inspector Andreou.'

Piers laughed. 'You must think I came down in the last shower.'

'I'm telling the truth. I went to see Andreou.'

Piers kicked the front door shut. Now they were alone in the hallway. 'And nobody else went with you?'

Erin shook her head. 'I went on my own.'

'You little liar.' A blob of spit flew from Piers's mouth and landed on Erin's chin.

'I'm telling the truth.'

'You're fucking fibbing. Nelson was in that interview room with you, wasn't he?' Piers's voice echoed in the hallway.

'Why would you say that?'

'Because I followed the pair of you from the police station. I saw him kiss your hand when you said goodbye. You cheating, lying slag!'

Erin swallowed hard. How did she miss that Piers had followed them? She'd been so engrossed in her conversation with Nelson that she'd forgotten who might have seen her. But then she'd done nothing wrong, other than walk alongside Nelson.

'I'm not cheating on you,' she said.

'But you did lie to me?'

Erin looked down at the silver chain around her ankle.

'Well?' Piers planted his hands on his hips. 'You lied about going to the police station with Nelson, didn't you?'

She stared at her polished toenails. *Temptation Red.*

'Didn't you?' Piers shouted, making Erin jump, but she continued to look down – this time at a spider making its way across the marble tiles.

'Well?' he yelled.

Erin nodded slowly before glancing up at Piers. His expression was victorious. He thought he'd won the fight. That was so important to Piers, Erin had learnt over the years. He always needed to be the one who was in the right.

'I haven't been unfaithful to you. I promise that nothing has happened between Nelson and me.'

Piers leant against the front door. It was a threat. A warning. He was blocking the only way out, shutting her in. 'It seems to me that your promises aren't worth very much.' His voice was calm and low. 'You lied about being at the police station with Nelson. Why wouldn't you lie about having an affair with him? Hardly going to admit it, are you?'

'I'm telling the truth. Nothing has happened between Nelson and me.' Erin could hear her heart pounding in her ears.

'Why should I believe you?'

Erin and Piers locked eyes with each other. Erin was searching for what to say, an answer that would satisfy Piers. But she knew there was no reply that he would accept. 'Because it's the truth. There's nothing more to say, except…' Erin's words trailed off.

'Except what?'

'Except,' she said. 'I have no more to give.'

Piers frowned. He looked shocked and confused. For once, he didn't have an immediate reply. He opened his mouth to speak, but no sound came out. He looked past Erin, searching for the words he needed, but instead he was distracted by a noise in the kitchen.

'Nai?' A Greek accent cut through the silence. It was the police officers on their shift, waiting for the call from the kidnappers, monitoring the phone line. Erin had forgotten all about them. Judging by his expression, so had Piers. His face softened, his body relaxed and he smiled with the same charm that had attracted her all those years ago. But it wasn't Erin he was smiling at. In that moment, it was as if she wasn't even in the room. Piers left his guard post at the front door and headed to the kitchen. She could hear him chatting to the Greek police officers, joking and laughing.

Erin needed to get out of there. She scanned the hallway. The keys to

Rosa's hire car dangled from a hook, alongside Vinnie's pork pie hat. She took a quick glance at Piers in the kitchen. He was engrossed in his conversation with the men, intent on impressing them. She grabbed the keys and checked on Piers one last time. He'd got out a couple of mugs and was heading for the coffee machine. It was a good moment to slip out.

Outside the villa, Rosa had parked her Fiat Punto at an angle, right alongside an olive tree. Erin guessed that she must've got out of the passenger side, because there wasn't enough room to open the driver's door. Erin did the same, hitched over the gear stick and slid across to the passenger seat.

At the T-junction with the mountain road, she had to wait five minutes for a shepherd to herd a flock of sheep. He was dressed in black trousers that ballooned around the thigh and long, leather boots like the ones that Andreou wore. The shepherd tipped his hat to thank Erin, showing a piece of black material tied around his brow.

The car door opened and Piers threw himself into the passenger seat. 'Where the hell do you think you're going?' he said.

Erin let out a screech. 'You made me jump!'

'Expecting someone else, were you? Rosa? Or more likely Nelson. Going for a romantic drive together, were you?'

'Actually, I was going for a drive on my own!' She slammed the car into first. 'To get away from you!'

'Spoiled that little plan, haven't I?'

Erin didn't answer. She swung the car left, around the hairpin bend, and headed out of town.

'Where are you taking me for this little day trip then?' Piers tried to kiss her cheek, but she lashed out and pushed his face away. 'That's not very nice,' he said. 'Only got kisses for Nelson nowadays?'

'Leave me alone.' Erin cried behind her sunglasses, forcing herself not to look across at Piers. She couldn't bear to give him the satisfaction. She slowed down by the disused chapel, the place where Zack was last seen. She swerved off the road causing Piers to slide out of his seat towards the windscreen.

'Steady on!' he said.

'Should've put your fucking seat belt on, shouldn't you?' Erin turned off the engine and strode off towards the chapel. Inside, she faced what would have once been the altar and sat cross-legged. She attempted to pray for Zack, but anger simmered in her chest. Eyes closed, she tried to focus, but her attention was taken by the sound of Piers walking in the grass, moving closer. 'Leave me alone!' she shouted out. 'I'm trying to pray for my son!'

Piers chuckled to himself and whistled something tuneless. Erin was livid. Any sense of peace she'd sought was ruined by him. She gave up and followed Piers back to the car.

'Hey!' she shouted after him. 'What's so bloody funny?'

'You make me laugh, stupid cow.' He sniggered. 'You and your prayers. Instead of praying for Zack, why don't you ask God to save your marriage? Fuck knows we need it after the way you've behaved.' Piers leant on the car bonnet.

'What does that mean?'

'You know exactly what I'm talking about.' Now he had his hand on the car door. 'Think about it.' Piers threw himself into the driver's seat and started the engine. Erin heard him crunch the car into gear and he was pulling away by the time she opened the back door.

'Going without me?' She slammed the car door shut.

'That's right. I'm giving up and carrying on without my wife.'

Erin climbed through the gap and flopped into the passenger seat. 'Where are you going now?'

Piers didn't answer. He shoved his foot on the accelerator, snatching through the gears and heading for the mountains.

'Where are you taking me?' Erin screamed.

'For a drive. Isn't that what you wanted?'

Tears stung Erin's eyes. She stared out at the fireflies swarming in the olive groves, the sun glistening on their lace wings. 'I've had enough of you,' she whispered, but Piers didn't hear.

'Isn't that where you were going with Nelson? For a drive?' Piers slammed the car into fifth gear.

Erin grabbed the door handle as Piers accelerated. 'Please can we go back to the villa now?'

Piers swung the Fiat Punto too tight into a hairpin bend, clipping the side of a whitewashed shrine on the verge and there was a clunk at the front of the car. 'Shit!' he said. 'Now look what you've made me do!'

He pulled over and examined the front bumper. 'No damage done, thank God!' He threw himself back in the driver's seat, but a candle in the shrine had tipped over, snuffing out the flame. He put his foot on the accelerator and took the next bend too quickly.

'Tell me,' he said. 'Seeing as you didn't have the decency to include me this morning, I want to know what the police had to say about Zack.'

Erin didn't reply.

'Talk to me!' Piers yelled.

Erin flinched. 'I've seen a photo of the suspected kidnappers.'

'What? You're talking in fucking code again. What are you going on about?'

'I'm telling you that Police Inspector Andreou showed me a photo of the suspected kidnappers this morning.'

'If that's the case, then why the hell don't they go and arrest the buggers? Maybe then they'll find Zack and we can go home, and get away from this godforsaken island.

'The police know who the kidnappers are, but they don't know where they're keeping Zack. The point is, that the photo links Zack's kidnappers with the Kos kidnappers I told you about.'

'Kos kidnappers? The ones who took a Dutch girl last year?'

'That's right.' Erin reached in her tote bag and pulled out a black and white photo. 'These are the Kos kidnappers,' she said. 'And your mate Reg is right here in the foreground.'

Piers slammed on the brakes and veered off the road. 'He's not my mate! I'd never met him before I came here on holiday. I've already told you that.'

'And look who else is there.' Erin pointed to the photo. 'Vinnie. Right here facing the camera. Now, you can't tell me that he's not your bloody mate.'

Piers snatched the photo from Erin.

'Don't you get it?' Erin said. 'Vinnie and Reg are tied up with this whole bloody people trafficking ring and with the people who've taken Zack. They're in it up to their necks.'

'They're fucking not! Where the hell did you get that idea from?' Piers threw the photo in Erin's face.

'The police.'

'Load of fucking rubbish.'

'This photo proves that they're involved. And you know what? Your mate Vinnie is right in the middle of the whole thing. He owes these people traffickers money, thousands and thousands of euros. He's refused to pay them and now these men are after Vinnie's blood.'

'Oh God, here we go. Your imagination is running riot again. I can tell you're a bloody writer. OK, so if that's the case, if these people traffickers are after his blood, then why didn't they just kill Vinnie?'

'Because they want their money!' Erin screamed. 'They've taken a boy hostage to get it back.' Erin bit her lip and forced back the tears. 'And now we know that they've got the wrong boy. It was Max they wanted to kidnap, not Zack.'

Piers shook his head. 'You're out of your fucking mind.' He slammed the car back into gear and drove on.

'You must have had some idea that Vinnie and Reg were involved in all of this crap.' She glanced across at Piers, but he wouldn't look her in the eye.

'You need your head looking at, if you ask me.' Piers glanced in the rear-view mirror at a moped pulling in close behind the car.

'Actually, my head is the clearest it's been in years. And for the record, you do know Reg. It was a lie that you'd never met him before. I overheard you talking to him last week.'

'Spying on me, were you?' Piers shook his fist at the moped as it overtook them.

'You know what else? You knew all about this situation. You brought us here on holiday, knowing that Vinnie owed those men money. You knew they wanted revenge and it was dangerous, but you still brought your family here and now Zack is paying for it.'

Piers slammed on the brakes and the car spun in a full circle, sending a swirl of dust into the air and finishing up facing down the mountain. Erin screamed and grabbed on to the sides of her seat.

'All right!' Piers yelled. 'I knew Vinnie was in a bit of trouble, but I didn't think that they'd bloody kidnap Zack, did I?' He reversed the car and drove back in the direction of the mountains.

'But you did know it was dangerous to come here?'

'I didn't think we'd be in danger, did I? How the fuck was I to know they'd get the wrong boy?'

A string of worry beads swung from the rear-view mirror, bobbing as they drove over bumps and potholes. Erin unhooked the beads and threaded them through her fingers, taking in the smoothness of the marble, the ripples in the stone. A crucifix, carved in marble, hung from where the thread had been tied. Erin pressed the cross between her fingers and began to pray for Zack. But again, Piers ruined her peace.

'What the fuck's your problem, Erin?' he said.

She clasped the worry beads in her fist and squeezed them until her knuckles turned white. 'You,' she said. 'You're my problem. My son has been kidnapped in a foreign land and you haven't supported me. You've been no use to me at all. In fact, I don't think you even love me anymore.' She loosened her fists around the worry beads. 'Maybe you never loved me.'

'Of course, I love you, Erin. You're my wife, for Christ's sake.'

Erin slipped the worry beads into her pocket and wound down the window. She closed her eyes and took in the mountain air, the scent of wild sage and lavender. 'Maybe I don't want to be your wife any more,' she whispered.

If there'd been a trace of shock in Piers's face, Erin might've taken the comment back. But an expression of amusement flicked in his eyes. 'Don't make me laugh. You'd never manage without me.'

'Yes, I would, I'd be fine.' Erin's hands were shaking.

'You're kidding yourself,' he snorted, 'You'd never manage on your own. You've got no way of earning your keep and you can't even control the only child you've got.'

'That's complete and utter crap. I managed just fine on my own before I met you. There's no reason why I couldn't do the same again.'

'I'd like to see you try. You couldn't find a job that would earn you anything like enough money. It'd be the end of those brands you love so much.' He nodded to Erin's trainers. 'But I'd be happy to put you up in some poxy little ex-council flat.' He smirked. 'I'd do that out of the kindness of my heart.'

Erin glanced down at her feet. Her shoes. Jimmy Choos. 'I'd rather be on my own for the rest of my life than have you watch every move I make.'

'Wish I was dead, do you?' Piers laughed.

Erin took a deep breath. 'I wish the world was flat and you'd walk off the edge of it.'

'I wouldn't dream of making it so easy for you.'

Silence.

Erin looked out at an old woman in a black headscarf, selling fruit by the side of the road. She fanned herself with a newspaper and raised her hand to them as they passed. Erin wanted to scream out of the window at the woman, tell her that she'd had enough of this life with Piers, that she needed to get away.

Piers took a cigarette from his pocket and lit up.

'Why have you gone back to the cigarettes?' Erin asked.

'I've started smoking since your bloody son went missing. So much for a sodding holiday. I've been stressed to hell and you've been all over the place. It's enough to drive anyone to drink. You should count yourself lucky that it's only fags.'

A bubble of anger burst in Erin's chest. 'You've been stressed? What do you think it's been like for me?' It's *my* son that's gone missing, you know. I'm the one who's going spare. As usual, you've been no bloody support whatsoever.'

'I have supported you! Christ, what more do you want from me?' Piers blew a smoke ring in Erin's face.

'You just don't understand how I feel.' Erin rested her head against the window and felt the vibration of the engine through her cheek. 'The only person who understands is Nelson.'

'Nelson?' Piers said, smirking. 'So, I am right about him. You do have something going on with him, don't you? The struggling artist and the failed writer getting it on together?'

'Don't be so bloody stupid.' Erin spoke through gritted teeth.

'You're having an affair with him, aren't you?' Piers yelled. He grabbed Erin's chin, forcing her to look at him. The Fiat careered onto the grass verge as Piers took his eyes off the road.

'Piers! Look where you're going! And you're hurting me. Stop it.'

'And you, little slut, are being unfaithful to me.' He squeezed her wrist, clamping it harder.

'Get off me!' Erin scrabbled around for the door handle. 'Let me out of the car.'

'What?'

'You heard me. Let me out of the car!'

Erin went for the handle and flung open the door. Piers stamped on the brakes and she stumbled out. Erin ran straight ahead. Piers killed the engine and she heard the car door slam. He was coming after her. She headed for an olive grove, running through the gnarled, ancient trees and sending the grazing sheep scuttling. She glanced over her shoulder and he was an arm stretch away. She ran on, gaining speed, but at the other side of the olive grove, she came to the edge of a cliff and an expanse of cloudless sky. There was nowhere to run. Piers caught up with her by a tumbledown shepherd's hut overlooking the sea.

'What the fuck's going on with you?' He grabbed her by the shoulders and shook her. 'Are you having an affair with Nelson? Tell me for God's sake.'

'Of course I'm bloody not.'

'I don't believe you. Lying slut. I can see how this whole thing has happened now. Zack goes missing, you get yourself in a right bloody state and fall into the arms of the first man who shows you a bit of sympathy.'

The sound of an engine whirred in the distance. A moped snaked its way up the mountain road towards the monastery. Piers glanced over his shoulder at the bike, loosened his grip and Erin wriggled free, escaping him, but with nowhere to run. They stood by the cliff edge, staring at each other in silence.

'Honestly, Piers. There's nothing going on with Nelson.'

'I don't fucking believe you!' Piers's eyes narrowed to slits. He shot out his right arm and grabbed Erin's neck, squeezing it tight and firm. Then both hands. Seconds passed, but it seemed like minutes. Erin's throat constricted. Her vision blurred. Pushing outwards, she tried to prise open his arms, but still Piers's hands were planted on her neck, throttling and gripping. She couldn't die like this, not at the hands of her husband. She had to fight back.

She rammed her fist underneath Piers's chin and his head jerked back. She heard a chink of his teeth and he spat a bead of blood onto his chin. Piers's lips moved but there was no sound. 'Bitch,' he mouthed, wiping the back of his hand across his bloodied chin. He lurched at Erin's neck again, but she took a step back and tripped on the scattered stones of the ruined shepherd's hut. She fell backwards. Piers grabbed at Erin's neck, but missed and landed right beside her. He fell heavily on his face, right on the jagged stones.

He clambered to his feet and that's when Erin saw that his right temple was gashed and his face was streaked with blood.

'You're hurt!' she said.

Piers raised a hand to his head, swayed and collapsed onto his back. Erin knelt beside him, examining his wounds and searching his face. There was no movement, only a blank stare. She bent in close, thinking he might be dead, but Piers blinked one slow blink. He was alive after all.

'I'll help you get up,' she said, but Piers shot out his hand and went for Erin's neck once more, squeezing her throat. He seemed to gain some inner strength and lurched forward, forcing her back, pinning her to the ground. With both hands around her neck, he strangled her, pressing hard. This was it. Piers was killing her.

Erin grabbed one of the sharp rocks and pounded it against her husband's temple. One, two, three times. Piers raised his right hand to his head and spat a spray of blood in Erin's face. He slumped onto his side, grabbing her arm, but she pushed him away, feeling the pulse in his wrist beat slower, weaker and slower still. Piers's hand fell away and his head flopped to one side. He lay motionless in the grass beside her. All was quiet, except for the sound of the bells tolling in the monastery across the bay.

Piers's lips were swollen, his cheeks streaked with blood, but his eyes were closed and his expression was peaceful. She opened her mouth to scream, but no sound came out. What the hell had she done? She beat her fists against her temples. What in God's name was she going to do?

She turned over her right hand. The bloodied rock sat in her palm. The murder weapon. She ran her fingers over the stone's sharp edges, smearing the blood on her fingers. Her husband's blood. She headed to the cliff, hurled the rock, and watched for the splash as it landed in the sea.

Erin inched closer to the cliff edge, shuffling forward until her toes were lined up with the sheer drop. Tears ran down her cheeks and gathered at her jawline, dripping onto her chest. She inched further forward, closer to the sea with the tips of her shoes hanging over the cliff. There was a fleeting temptation to take the final step. But somewhere out there, on this rugged island, Zack was waiting for her to save him and there was nobody who would search for him in the way she would. Erin glanced down at the waves pummelling the beach below and shuffled back from the edge.

Over her shoulder, Piers lay in the grass. The murder weapon was gone, but her husband still lay by the shepherd's hut. She threaded her way back through the rough grass and crouched over his body. Touching his head with light fingers, she examined his wounds: the cut on his brow, the gash on his temple, the split in his lip. Her heart rose and fell. She couldn't believe that she'd murdered him. Covering her face with her hands, she sobbed, her shoulders shaking. She wiped away her tears and stared at her husband. She had to pull herself together, she needed to think straight.

Kneeling beside Piers, she rammed her hands under his side and rolled him onto his face. She gasped. The hair on the back of Piers's head was matted with blood. A wave of nausea drifted over her chest. She couldn't bear the sight. Taking fistfuls of his shirt she pulled her husband onto his back. Grass and earth now stuck to the blood on his face and gathered at the corners of his mouth. Erin grabbed Piers's calves and tugged, dragging his body, straining to move him. Piers was muscled and broad, a struggle for her to shift. But slowly, inch by inch, she slid his body along the grass until it was lined up with the cliff edge.

There his body lay, ready for the final push, his burial in the sea. Erin recovered for a few seconds, resting her shaky hands on her hips. She pulled the worry beads from her pocket, closed her eyes and fell to her knees. Her lips moved, but she didn't speak. It was a final prayer, the last rites for her husband, but the prayer was fleeting.

Erin flicked her hair from her eyes and bent over Piers's body. His face was pale, his skin dull and waxy-looking. His hands were tanned from the days on Symi, but half-moons of dirt were lodged under his fingernails from where he'd clawed at the ground in the moments before he died.

This was it. This was the end. Ten years of marriage finished here on this clifftop in Greece.

Erin planted her palms under Piers's side. But there was a peace about him that stopped her. Something in the upturn at the corner of his mouth reminded her of when they'd first met, the charm in his smile, the warmth of their first kiss. She bent in closer, examining the creases around his eyes, the curl of his eyelashes, the scar on his chin. She breathed in the familiar scent of his cologne, mixed with sweat and blood. Now closer still, their noses nearly touched, and as her lips almost met his, Piers opened his eyes.

LIN LE VERSHA

Lin Le Versha has drawn on her experience in London and Surrey schools and colleges as the setting for her debut crime novel. She has written over twenty plays and published two non-fiction books. She now lives on the Suffolk coast and is Director of Southwold Arts Festival.

linleversha@hotmail.com

A Level in Murder

CHAPTER ONE – EDMUND

We move apart and lie side by side on the rumpled sheets. I turn my pillow over. It cools my neck. The August sun knifes through the gap in the dusty maroon curtains that don't quite reach the sill – the blade slicing the dust on the chest of drawers around her old perfume bottles.

She shifts. The bed springs creak.

'How about a cup of tea?' I ask.

'Or we could...' she touches me – there. I slide away from her. I sit on the side of the bed. She strokes my back. She pulls me back down.

We lie. Silent. A spider spins a thread from the lampshade in the afternoon sunlight. She reaches for my hand. Pulls me towards her. Her finger traces the path left by a bead of sweat on my chest. She leans over, catches it on the tip of her tongue.

Lying back, she sighs. 'Yes, tea would be lovely.'

I pull on my boxers, reach for my shirt.

'I'll stay here for a while. You should be working.' She pulls the covers up.

I feel her watching as I tug on my trousers. I turn. She yawns, stretches luxuriously. I pick up her faded yellow silk kimono. I hand it to her.

Sitting up, she takes it, covers her breasts. 'Changed my mind. I'll get up and make supper. Spaghetti Bolognese?'

'Yes, please, Mummy.'

CHAPTER TWO – STEPH

Derek peed on a rosebush. A prize Queen Elizabeth with the most delicate shell pink blooms. Steph looked around. No one witnessed it. She'd banned Derek from Southwold beach after he'd watered the pale blue handbag of a lady watching the sunset with her fisherman boyfriend. How ridiculous – a blue leather handbag on the beach.

'It's the streets for you until we have the beach to ourselves again.'

She fled up the road in case someone overheard her and concluded it was she, not her dog, who was barking. It had been a glorious summer – her first in Oakwood. Weeks of endless blue-sky days and barbeques. Suffolk had been more like Portugal or Italy. Even the east wind had moved out for a few weeks in the solid heat. Bees and butterflies had basked in the endless sunshine, but so had the vicious mosquitoes.

'Ouch! Shitting Henry!' she gasped, as the mozzy bite on the back of her heel became unbearable. She tugged Derek to a stop and told him to sit. He ignored her. She bent down and dug her nail into the swollen lump, attempting to release the maddening gunge injected there.

'Oy! Missus! Your dog peed on my statue! Get him off!'

A grumpy-looking man had been dead-heading the yellow roses on a trellis by his front door. He limped towards her, waving his secateurs.

'I'm so sorry.'

Steph pulled Derek away from the concrete gargoyle-fairy.

'He should be on a short lead if you can't control him.'

Steph dragged Derek away from the other concrete slab, which resembled a squashed rabbit. Two weeks ago, she'd moved into the ground-floor flat of an Edwardian house with a small garden opening onto fields. The moment she saw Derek at the RSPCA, a black and white collie-lurcher, she knew she'd found her ideal dog. She'd never trained a dog, and Derek had never been trained. She now kept him on a lead to avoid blue handbag incidents.

The sharp lemon tang of gin and tonic tempted her to return to her flat. She'd go the long way home. A police car siren in the distance pushed images of her leaving do into her head. She replayed the pathetic affair – a few drinks with a few colleagues. After almost thirty years in the police force, it should have been a bigger party. But they don't celebrate the careers of broken people.

The spiral started. Her stomach heaved. Panic gripped her. She breathed in, counting to seven, held her breath, then let it go. She repeated the exercise she'd been taught, while concentrating on the number of the small panes in a circular gable window. The disrupting images ejected, she breathed out. Oakwood was a new beginning – a fresh start.

The mix of Tudor, Georgian and Dutch-gabled houses led to the High Street. It could be any high street anywhere. Tesco, Joules and Costa Coffee had replaced the independent shops selling antiques, local pottery and farm produce. She used to drive from Ipswich at the weekends, looking for unusual presents in the little old-fashioned shops. Now she lived here, they'd disappeared.

A midnight blue silk dress caught her eye in the window of Miranda Modes, where she'd bought her new 'ensembles' – the posh saleswoman's word for outfits. Steph felt fourteen again under her appraising gaze. She emerged with five brightly coloured outfits, one for each working day, she would never have chosen by herself.

After slobbing around in black tops and jeans for almost a year, she could hardly believe the transformation. Her blonde hair reshaped into a short, spiky style made her look younger than fifty-three. She had a fresh glow. Her doughy skin, developed over the months being housebound, had brightened in the summer sunshine. She would need a second mortgage to pay off her credit card, but it was worth it. Even after a few days, she was enjoying her job as the College Receptionist in her new school uniforms.

Derek crouched down low, in attack mode. A tall woman, who appeared to be wearing a long nightdress and walking with a white fluffy cushion on a pink string, floated towards them.

'Hello, Steph – and what's your name?' The woman ruffled Derek behind his ears.

'Derek. Sorry I don't...' mumbled Steph.

'You won't know us all yet – I'm Caroline, Head of Art.'

'Is she a Scottie?'

'No. Norfolk Terrier, aren't you, Marlene? Heading for the common?'

Steph smiled and nodded as Caroline chatted on.

'Such a relief to get out. My partner's driving me bonkers! You know, Margaret Durrant, music teacher?'

Steph wasn't sure. Over the last few days, she'd met about a hundred and fifty teachers and members of support staff. She listened carefully for any clues to identify Caroline's partner.

'Anyway, Margaret's had another row with Harriet, her boss.'

'Really?'

'Margaret was Director of Music, then a year ago, she found out she had Parkinson's.'

'Oh, I'm sorry.'

'She reduced her timetable and Harriet Weston took over. Marlene! Stop doing that to Derek!'

'Can we let them off here?'

Liberated, Derek and Marlene bounced off into the dusty bracken, on the trail of some irresistible rabbit or fox smell. They chased around, leaping over a fallen silver birch tree, in and out of the clumps of ferns, the edges rusty with the first signs of autumn.

'Anyway, the latest row is about changing the timetable for some brilliant cellist.'

Not sure how to react, Steph fixed on a sympathetic smile while nodding in time to Caroline's complaints. They stood side by side as the dogs dashed through the undergrowth in the watery evening sunshine.

'Gosh – is that the time? Margaret will moan if I'm late for supper. Lovely to chat. Come on, Marlene – MARLENE!'

As Caroline hooked Marlene on her lead and scurried away, Steph saw that what she thought was a nightdress was an elegant, pink dress in some floaty material. Miranda Modes' saleswoman would have approved of her style.

The day had drained. The sun had disappeared behind the silver birches, leaving a grey-pink smear across the sky. An early start tomorrow. It was the first day of lessons for the students after three days of enrolment. She turned towards home and supper – intending to avoid the drinks cupboard.

CHAPTER THREE – EDMUND

I read it again. Is that first page too shocking? I want you to be there, alongside me. I've polished it as a novelist might, so you can experience every moment with me. I have a unique story to share with you. Home educated, allowed to work on my talent without being distracted by school. Now I'm ready. Ready to step on the stage as a professional cellist. Since I was four years old Mother and I have been preparing for this moment.

In *A Life Worth Sharing – Write Your Memoir in 60 days*, JM Rowe suggests opening with 'a hook – a piece describing a powerful event at the centre of your life story.' Is this the JM Rowe hook? I see my memoir on a bookshop table. You walk in out of the rain, in your lunch hour. You pick up my book, my story, and flutter through it. Casually, you read the first page. You reach the last line, you gasp! You're hooked. Rowe's right. It stays.

Mother calls our special love 'cuddles'. She needs them more now. Now I'm at college. You must wonder about my father? He's gone. He left. I'm not sure why. She won't talk about it and goes quiet if I mention him. I can only remember a gigantic shadow with no features. Sometimes I wish I could get to know him. Mother was a concert pianist. Then she had me and stopped. She married him but didn't forgive him. After he left, I woke in her bed.

For the last thirteen years we've had a rigid routine. It makes me feel safe. We plan our days – English, maths, history, geography, music theory and practice, practice, practice, five hours' cello practice every day. I breathe my cello. I feel I'm most me when I play it.

I passed all my cello exams with Distinction. We'd wait apart from the other children in music teachers' dining rooms, which often smelled of yesterday's cabbage. After my performance, their eyes followed me. Mother said, 'They think it's a CD they heard through the closed door.' But she's always so positive.

I started playing at music festivals when I was six. Again, I sat alone with Mother. The other children giggled, chatted and complained about their music teachers. We just waited. No distractions. We usually won – actually, that's not quite true – we always won.

You think I had a lonely childhood? Not at all. I had Mother with me all the time and I had my cello and my music. Now, as I take this next step, I'd like to share my story with you. This is my 'daybook' where, according to Rowe, 'I can reflect on the past and record present thoughts and experiences.'

'Edmund Fitzgerald takes the technical demands for granted and has a vibrant abandonment that makes his music passionate and truly individual. At seventeen, he is a genius cellist in the making.' First place – English Young Musicians' Festival.

I was the youngest competitor, beating some excellent musicians, most of them graduates from music conservatoires. As I walked on that stage, I was so nervous, but once I started playing, I lived inside the music. It's always like that.

I met Harriet Weston, one of the judges who gave me first place, when she came down from the stage to congratulate me. 'You can win BBC Young Musician next year, you know.' I was overwhelmed. Me? BBC Young Musician? 'I've coached others in the past...' She reeled off the names of two finalists and one winner.

Mother stood up, brushed down her skirt, steadied her handbag on her left arm, like the Queen. 'I agree. Edmund's close, but not quite ready yet.'

They talked about me. I stood beside them. Taller than both. They made it clear, shoulders turned inward, that I was to be silent. Mother and Harriet negotiated my future while I stood and said nothing. I felt flattered and stupid at the same time.

Harriet – she insisted on Harriet – said I should enrol at Oakwood Sixth Form College, where she was Director of Music, to take A Levels. With my outstanding performance, they would be my passport to The Royal College of Music.

'Edmund needs to maintain his practice regime.' Mother lifted her handbag further up her body. Harriet held her ground.

'All music students have access to practice rooms, so Edmund may do several hours' practice each day under my supervision and the rest with you.'

Harriet Weston again dangled BBC Young Musician – a tasty morsel before a shark. In her grey blue suit. (Did I really write that? Mother a shark?) 'Think about it and let me know when you've decided.' She handed a card to Mother. The handbag jaws snapped shut. She nudged me away. I clutched the trophy as we left, not sure what would happen. I had to wait until Mother decided.

That night Mother needed long cuddles.

College was scary. Yes, eventually Mother agreed to what she called my 'incessant pestering'. I asked her for jeans and a top with a hood. I know that's what they wear, I've seen them from my bedroom window. Mother said 'No'. Said I'm different. Do I want to be different? I suppose I do.

Rowe advises recreating specific moments for your reader. 'Reproduce speeches and scenes so the reader can share your life with you.' My first week at college had lots of those moments.

I felt very different as I walked into the enormous oak hall for enrolment. It smelled of floor polish. The old floor was shiny – a wooden mirror. Little crowds squealed and hugged each other – they peered at results slips. I don't have any GCSE results. My head ached. It was much quieter at home. I stood alone. Had I made the most dreadful mistake? I turned around to go back through the door – back home to Mother. I felt sick – my stomach churned. Where was the loo?

They all looked at me. I felt their eyes as they pretended not to look. They'd never seen me before. They all knew each other. The same school, the same football team, the same street corners. They were confident and bouncy and shouty. I'm so different.

Harriet smiled as she walked towards me across the gleaming hall floor. I enjoyed feeling different then. I felt so special. She had the look of being looked at. Tutors sitting at their desks around the edge of the hall stopped writing, turned away from talking to a student or just stared as she walked, no floated, down the length of the hall. I was so happy to see her.

Looking at the groups of students, she leant across and said, 'Don't be nervous, all the other students are feeling the same. That's why they squeal so much to show they aren't.'

I must have looked scared or something as she said, 'Don't worry that you haven't got results slips. You've got a great talent.'

I said the other teachers might not agree with her. At that she touched my shoulder (my nerves tingle in that place now, as I remember her touch) and said that she would be with me and not to worry.

Across the hall was a desk with a printed notice dangling from the front of it saying, 'All English Courses – David Stoppard'. Behind it sat a well-built man with a black beard that looked like it had been charcoaled on. He ran all the teachers in English – apparently they're called 'Departments'. While Harriet explained why I had taken no exams, what an outstanding cellist I was and how well I would do on his course, he beamed at her, never lowering his eyes. He had that Red Riding Hood wolf's grin and looked as if he'd like to eat her up.

'Call me David' was so helpful. When I told him I enjoyed Dickens, Hardy and Austen, he laughed and said that I was better read than some of his new teachers! I don't think I can be.

With that, in the beam of David's gaze, she guided me to a desk at the far end of the hall labelled 'Sam Griffiths – Performing Arts'. Very different to David, Sam had a tiny face and all his clothes were black. The sunlight showed up the gaps in his thin blond hair and the sweat marks under his arms. He wasn't much older than me. He looked a little scruffy, not what I'd imagined a teacher to look like. Harriet recited my history once again. Sam looked terrified under her gaze. He pushed a form at me, which I signed, and gave me a list of plays. I thanked him and we walked to the Music A Level desk.

The old lady sitting there frowned as we approached. Harriet spoke loudly, 'Edmund, this is Margaret Durrant, who will teach you theory.' Margaret sniffed into a tissue, which she tucked up her sleeve. She turned a list round so it faced us, I signed in the bottom space.

'Thanks for standing in for me. I need to get Edmund settled.'

Margaret sniffed and looked irritated. 'That's fine, Harriet.' She didn't think it was fine at all.

We left quickly. I felt safe – happy in her glow. She steered me towards the Music Centre by touching my shoulder again. I liked that. I didn't mind people looking at us together. The Music Centre, a modern concrete building, has two classrooms on the right and two practice rooms on the left. At the end of the corridor an impressive recital room can seat about two hundred and fifty people, and beyond that is an enormous classroom with a recording studio. Harriet told me to meet her there with my cello at ten o'clock the next day.

At home, I told Mother about my day. I shared the enrolling, the Music Centre and the teachers – or tutors they're called. I didn't tell her how nervous I was. Or how noisy the college was. Or how it felt to be stared at like a fascinating specimen in a bottle. I've decided that I can cope with college if I go to my lessons, stay in the practice room and not go to the canteen.

With my cello strapped on my back, I felt more confident climbing up the hill on my second day. It didn't seem as steep. I went across Main Quad to the Music Centre, the way Harriet had taken me, so I didn't get lost and have to ask.

Harriet was waiting for me. Handing me a swipe card with my photo and signature already on it, she said, 'It opens the front door so you can get into the Music Centre any time to practise.' Then she gave me to a girl called Justine in Year 13, who was in one of the practice rooms, playing her violin. It sounded rather good. Harriet asked her to show me around college and said we could practise all morning.

I think of Justine as I write this now and feel happy. I'm reminded of that picture of Ophelia in my encyclopaedia – the one of her floating in the stream and covered in reeds and weeds and herbs. Justine's like that, but she has masses of bright red curls – Pre-Raphaelite red.

That morning was wonderful. For the first time I felt me, without Harriet or Mother being there. Justine suggested we spent the morning practising. She showed me the Bach sonata she was working on.

'You play it and I'll listen.'

She played it very well. When she'd finished, I clapped, and she made an elegant bow. We laughed.

'That was lovely. Why haven't we met at music festivals?'

She lowered her head, looked at me out of the corner of her eye. 'I wasn't good enough.'

'That's not true.'

'It was until Harriet helped me. I'm pleased you like it.'

'Your intonation is great, but...'

'But? Go on.'

'You could lean a little more into those embellishments.'

'You mean the trills?'

'Yes, emphasise the turns and appoggiaturas.' I grabbed my cello. 'Shall I show you how to make them sit on top of the tune – like decorations?'

She sat beside me on the double piano stool. I was so close to her face that when I turned to talk to her, I thought we'd touch. I could smell rosemary; it must have been her shampoo; fresh and gentle like her. 'Now concentrate on my left hand, my third and fourth fingers.' She moved closer. The smell of rosemary was stronger. I pictured her washing her hair. I turned the picture off so I could concentrate. I played an extract and showed her how to weave in the delicate ornaments to create the effect Bach intended.

'Let me try it.'

She picked up from the section where she'd had a slight tumble. This time she ran into the turns and trills with no hesitation.

'You see – easy, isn't it?'

'Now it's your turn.' She sat on the edge of the small table to listen.

I closed my eyes and was about to play the opening notes, when the door swung open and hit the wall. A boy – Jack or Jake, I think he's called – crashed into the room. He stood still when he saw us together and looked puzzled.

'I've come to take Justine to the canteen.'

He's spotty and has dandruff. They walked off to the canteen holding hands. They didn't ask me. I left college.

That night the picture of Justine so close to my face kept coming into my head. We would make a splendid duo. I've written a list of pieces we can play. I'll ask her if she'd like to rehearse with me after the concert – after I've heard her perform in public. I don't want to make a mistake. I've decided not to tell Mother.

That first week I spent all my free time in the Music Centre practising. I felt safe there, I belonged. Harriet Weston was there whenever I was. When she accompanied me, we fitted together perfectly. She suggested a stress on that note, to hold back on that phrase, to make a dramatic crescendo in that section. She was so right. Mother is technically sound, but Harriet has the ear of a performer. Each day the Elgar moved to a new level. I grew with her coaching. She had so much time for me. I adore her!

Other students would stand at the door, listen to us, then leave. Harriet took no notice of them. They realised they were not to intrude. Justine stood. She listened for a while, then opened the door and asked for a time to practise with Harriet for the concert. Harriet gestured to me, 'Sorry Justine, not now, you can see we're in the middle of this challenging passage.' Justine paused, then left, looking sad.

The next day she returned. This time Harriet went to the door and said, 'Sorry Justine, I'm up to my neck at the moment. Margaret's said she'd love to accompany you and she has masses of time. She'll see you whenever you like.' Harriet looked irritated and her voice was sharp. Justine eyes looked watery. I was unhappy that I was the reason for her sadness. I hoped she wouldn't blame me. But, having found Harriet, I didn't want her to get off the piano stool. I wanted my piece to be a triumph at the Enrolment Concert.

CHAPTER FOUR – STEPH

'Bye Miss, have a good weekend!' Five students walked past the Reception desk out into the sunshine, chatting about their plans for the weekend. 'You're joking! He did what?' squealed the Goth girl. The sliding doors cut off further information on his shocking behaviour.

Steph grimaced as she pulled off her right shoe. Her feet were killing her. She'd been standing all day. The left one took longer to peel off. Her feet breathed a sigh of relief as they were freed at last. She'd made it. The end of her first week.

Most of the students had trooped past to catch their buses or walk down the hill home. The tutors, after a week of enrolling about a thousand students and meeting their new classes, had also taken advantage of the sunny Friday afternoon to leave early. An hour to go and she'd be able to join them – assuming she could get her shoes on again.

Three students stopped by the desk. A dark-haired boy wearing a grey hoodie leant over and asked, 'Have you found a black backpack, please? It's got my computer coursework in it.'

She opened the door of the lost property cupboard. 'Sorry, no black bags. I hope you find it.'

'Thanks, Miss. It'll probably turn up.' He strolled off, blasé about his lost work.

Ben Bryant, the Principal, opened his office door behind the Reception desk and stood beside her. 'Well done! A good week. Are you coming back for the Enrolment Concert this evening?'

Steph had photocopied the programmes so knew it was happening but had no idea she was expected to attend. She had planned a night in front of a box set away from the constant noise and endless questions of students and staff. But she didn't want to give the wrong impression. She held eye contact with Ben, so he didn't notice her bare feet.

'Remind me, what time does it start, please?'

'Seven thirty. I'll save you a seat if you like. Harriet Weston's transformed our concerts over the last year.'

'Really? Sounds like a good evening.'

'Good. See you in the Music Centre later. Why don't you turn the phones off now and go? It's been a long week.' With that, he tossed his car keys in the air, caught them and walked out of the sliding doors into the car park.

While she was fiddling with the complicated phone switches, a waft of Jo Malone perfume made her raise her head. Harriet Weston held out an A4 printed sheet.

'I know this is short notice and you've already done the photocopying, but I've had to make a change to this evening's concert. Would you mind popping this through your photocopier please? Two hundred and fifty, double-sided.'

'Shall I bring them over when they're done?'

'I'll hang on, if that's OK?'

Steph stepped back, set up the photocopier and watched Harriet, in her designer stiletto heels, click across the wooden floor. She looked so elegant, in a skin-tight black dress, worth at least a month's salary and proved she must live on lettuce – without the dressing. Sat on one of the black leather sofas, Harriet flicked through the local newspaper, left on the coffee table for visitors.

'It's not fair! I should play the finale. Not him!'

A cascade of bright red curls, on top of an emerald green silk dress, rushed at Harriet, who patted the space beside her on the sofa. The student shook her head and remained standing, a soggy tissue grasped in her hand, her mascara dripping from her eyelashes. She burst into tears.

'Now calm down, Justine.'

The student's sobs became quieter. Justine looked a mess. Swollen eyes, a dripping nose, and trembling lips contrasted with her stylish gown. Steph dithered, unsure if she had the right to intervene. Just as she was about to ask them to move from Reception, she was aware of someone standing in the shadow outside the Meeting Room door. It was Margaret Durrant. She kept out of Harriet's eyeline and listened to the exchange. Breathing deeply, Steph decided not to interfere and retreated to the photocopier to concentrate on the papers flipping into the tray.

'I should have spoken to you earlier, but I've decided that Edmund will play last tonight.'

'It's not fair!'

'Margaret told you, didn't she?'

'But I'm the best in Year 13 – it should be me!'

'You'll open the concert and play before him – two pieces to his one.'

At last Justine got her breathing under control. 'He's good but...'

'No buts – that's my decision.'

Justine flopped down beside Harriet. She handed Justine a tissue from the box on the table.

Justine blew her nose loudly. 'Last year you told me I was the best you'd ever worked with. Now you spend all your time working with him.'

'Look, he's home schooled and finding college a real struggle.'

'We were so close – until Edmund came.' She paused, sneaked a look at Harriet, then sat up straight. 'You also spend a lot of time with that new English teacher, David Stoppard.'

Harriet stared ahead.

Justine continued, 'Mr Weston's away at the moment, isn't he?'

'What's that supposed to mean?'

'Nothing really. Just that it'd be a shame if Mr Weston found out about David Stoppard.'

'Right – off you go, Justine. Splash cold water over your face and next time use waterproof mascara, darling.'

Horrified, Steph gasped at this vicious comment and the shocking exchange. Surely this wasn't how teachers and students talked to each other now? It didn't sound like the conversations she'd had with her teachers.

As Justine ran down the corridor, Margaret positioned herself in front of Harriet so she couldn't get off the sofa without pushing her out of the way. 'That was so cruel. You had no intention of telling that poor girl, did you?'

'I didn't need to. You did it for me. How dare you interfere!'

'Justine's worked hard and deserves to play last. Now you've got your ambitious claws into our new musical genius, she's last year's model, isn't she?'

'I couldn't care less what you think. It's my decision, and that's final.' Harriet got up, shoved Margaret out of her way, then turned to face her. 'I can get rid of you like that!' She clicked her fingers in Margaret's face. 'You should accept your illness and retire before the Principal has to ask you to leave.'

Harriet snatched the pile of programmes off the desk and marched out of Reception.

'You'll regret this, I promise you!' Margaret screamed at Harriet's back.

LISSA PELZER

Lissa Pelzer is a Patricia Highsmith fanatic based in Southern Germany. She has degrees in Anthropology and Psychology and is interested in using crime fiction to explore economic privilege and disadvantage, and the performance of gender and sexuality.

lissa.e.pelzer@gmail.com

The Personal Liar

CHAPTER ONE

Even in a crowd of good-looking people at the fashionable, rooftop beach bar, Markus Mayer stood out. Deeply tanned, supremely confident and with a body shaped by expensive outdoor hobbies, Peter spotted him immediately. But even without these attributes he would have known who Tina was talking about. As Markus moved between the various sunloungers, the pack swarmed around, not always looking at him but subtly keeping him at their core.

'He's from the Mayer family,' Tina said in English raising her eyebrows as far as her Botox forehead allowed. 'You know the Mayers.'

Peter didn't but he did know Stuttgart was full of families, the owners and heirs to automobile and washing machine fortunes.

'You should go over and introduce yourself. He was complaining today about the trainee positions intake at the Mayer Company, needing to find candidates before he can do his Instagram tour. I thought, who do I know who desperately needs to find a real job, a nice young educated man who'd fit right in at the Mayer Company?' She hooked a finger over her sunglasses and pulled them down her nose.

'Thank you.'

'He'd prefer personal contacts, of course. All these *Mittlestand* companies do. And if you advertise online these days you get thousands of applications, *thousands*. It's like a plague of locusts and... *es bringt nichts*!'

'You mean, it's not worth it,' Peter said.

'Exactly! Oh, darling, your German is getting so good. You should introduce yourself to him in German. Tell him your degree is Business and from England, but do it in German. That'll charm him.' She took a sip of her syrupy Cosmopolitan and her expensive red lipstick left a gooey smudge on the Martini glass. 'So, off you go.'

Peter shifted in his deckchair. He did *desperately* want to find a job, something that would lead to a career. Working six nights a week at the

Irish Pub and living in the same apartment as his manager was making him pretty miserable. But despite Tina's good intentions, Peter wasn't sure this was the best way to secure one.

'Is now really the place to go up to a stranger and ask about a job? I mean, he's at a beach bar on a Friday afternoon and he's drinking champagne with his friends.'

'Oh Peter, this is exactly when and how we Germans get business done. You need to be more direct and stop being so British!'

Peter shaded his eyes with his hand as he looked at the group, laughing and jumping around. They were roughly the same age as him but seemed more carefree. 'If we were somewhere else,' he said, 'at a party or at a private event, if there weren't so many people around, if the music wasn't so loud...'

'And do you spend much time in such places, running into people like Markus Mayer?'

'If I could afford to, I would.'

Tina tutted. 'Just don't complain to me again that I didn't give you the job at Gelber Sack if you won't even cross the sand for this one.'

Peter looked back towards where Markus Mayer was standing. Two women in bikinis were leaning into him for selfies but two men behind them kept photobombing and Peter could tell Markus didn't find it funny. Another young woman in a white bikini stood there too as if she were waiting her turn for a photo. It was as if he were a celebrity and it was a free-for-all. Peter watched as a slight crease travelled across Markus's serious forehead and his lips flexed in and out of his camera-ready smile. He saw the contempt Markus had for these fans. Peter knew he didn't want to do anything stupid or embarrassing around Markus. Just the thought of it turned him inside out. But Tina was right. If he could just go over there and introduce himself, say he'd heard about the positions and tell Markus he had a business degree, maybe he really would get a job out of this.

'Fine,' he said. 'I'll do it.' He clutched at the frame of the deckchair and quickly pushed himself to his feet before he could change his mind. Standing up, Peter wasn't any more confident, only a lot hotter out of the shade of the parasol. He gazed across at the Mercedes star on top of the Hauptbahnhof rotating slowly in the sunshine and the vineyards towards Esslingen shimmering like green velvet corduroy. Seeing the city below the rooftop bar, Peter felt something like vertigo but he thought of the company job and leaving the bar and took a lungful of air and stepped out.

The sand slid between his feet and his flip-flops and Peter walked inelegantly towards the group. Markus was sitting on the edge of a white, curtained bed now, his chest shone with freshly applied sunscreen and his champagne glass was set aside. Peter was just a couple of metres away and took a step forward. He opened his mouth to speak.

'*Vorsicht!*' someone called out.

Peter twisted his head just in time to see a volleyball flying towards him. His hands sprung up and he caught it, amazingly, but clumsily taking the full force of the impact in his shoulder. He looked at where the ball had come from and saw the blonde woman in the white bikini standing there. She glared at Peter as if *he'd* done something wrong.

Peter threw the ball back. '*Bitteschön,*' he said.

The woman didn't reply but continued to stare at him. Peter turned back towards Markus.

'*Vorsicht!*' came the call again.

Peter flinched, annoyed now. He lifted his hands but this time the ball flew past him. It landed with a loud slap in Markus Mayer's hands but hardly interrupted his smile. Peter watched as Markus moved the ball to one hand and threw it back with a confident flick of the wrist.

'*Dankeschön!*' the blonde called out and she sashayed across the sand towards Markus. 'I'm so clumsy!'

She stood there then between him and Markus. Her tanned skin and long blonde hair acting like an impenetrable barrier. She started making small talk and Peter rolled his eyes. She'd thrown that foul ball on purpose, Peter thought, and the first time too just to get to talk to him. The ploy was cringeworthy and transparent, but he couldn't be overly judgemental. After all, he was trying to talk to Markus too. It was only a shame he didn't have her attributes to use.

Peter hung on for a moment, letting the wisps of her dull conversation reach him. She was talking about clothes and people. Nothing interesting. Peter crossed his arms over his chest. Perhaps she'd wander off in a minute if she didn't get any attention and then he could step in. He glanced back at Tina and saw her peering over the back of a deckchair. Tina lifted her hand and waved him forward encouragingly as if he were a child in a school play. Peter turned back to Markus and he saw he was looking right at him. There was a questioning tilt to his head and his line of sight travelled towards Tina.

Peter turned away quickly, but just as he did a waiter with a tray full of drinks walked out. Peter backed up to avoid him, his heel kicked the base of the bed and he sat down. The phone flashed three times and Peter realised he was in the frame. Not only that but he was looking down the lens and smiling almost. He sprung from the bed and crossed the sand back to where Tina sat, laughing behind her hand.

'What on earth was that about?'

Peter could feel the blood rising to his face but tried to subdue it, to breathe through it and act calmly. 'It was a waste of time,' he said, bending over for his messenger bag. 'Too busy, too many people... If that's how Germans do it I don't know how they ever manage to get anything done.'

'Oh Peter...'

Tina paid the bill and they stood up and crossed towards where the beach ended and the rooftop parking began. The sand was hot and Tina complained, forcing Peter to hold his arm out to help her walk. He didn't look back but he hoped he was doing it in a way that suggested she was an aunt and nothing more if anyone were looking.

'Anyway, darling,' she said clutching his arm. 'As it's early I'll head back to the office and get some work done. You can find a taxi, can't you?' She pressed a twenty euro note into his hand.

'I'll get one from the Hauptbahnhof.'

'Lovely. Well then. I'll call you. Maybe we can have lunch next week.'

'And if Markus Mayer comes back into the office...'

'What?' Tina asked, taking her key from her bag and pressing the button. Somewhere under the roof, her small Mercedes beeped.

'The trainee positions.'

'Oh, yes. Yes.' She leaned towards him and Peter kissed her cheek, felt her twisting slightly bringing her lips towards his. 'Have fun at work.'

'I will,' he said, although he knew he wouldn't.

CHAPTER TWO

At the sound of the bar door opening, Peter turned sharply, one foot in his trainer, the other still in the flip-flop. Oliver stood over him, his stomach pressing against the waistcoat Oliver wore identifying him as the pub manager.

'You're late,' he said in German. 'Again!'

Peter grabbed his other shoe and, using the shelf for support, forced his foot inside. He looked up at the backroom clock and saw it was ten minutes after five.

'You're habitually late.'

He hadn't taken a taxi with the money Tina had given him and had instead laid out at the park in front of the Neues Schloss, worked on his tan and thought about things. He'd tried to imagine a scenario in which he met Markus Mayer and discussed the trainee positions. He would run into him at the library, perhaps, although Markus didn't look like the book type. Or he'd see him in a café, but Peter rarely went to cafés and when he did, he was with Tina. So no matter what scenario he imagined, Peter couldn't picture a world where Markus would talk to him, where he would see him as a contemporary. And even worse, he was worried Markus might recognise him from that accidental photobomb and be suspicious.

'Peter?'

'Sorry?'

From behind the bar door, a loud crash sounded, not like a glass hitting the floor but more like a whole shelf full.

'What the fuck, now?' Oliver pushed past him, sending him against the table and Peter stayed there for a moment before following Oliver through to the bar.

The Irish Pub was a small basement place, dark and woody. A large mirror ran along behind the bottles. Beneath this, there was usually a counter, but it had collapsed taking down a rack of glasses.

'You were sitting on it!' Oliver yelled at Ian, the only Irish person in the bar.

'I never was!' Ian pushed his hand through his black hair. 'The counter was rotten. It was ready to go sooner or later.'

'I don't care, just get it cleaned up, both of you.'

Peter got down and began picking up the larger shards of glass while Ian went for the broom. Someone was waiting to be served and Oliver huffed down the gangway. On his hands and knees, Ian caught Peter's gaze and rolled his eyes.

'He's twitchy at the moment,' Ian whispered. 'Been ordering coke online and not just for himself. He stuck a fake name above his own on the pub's bell today, got a parcel and then took the paper off again.'

Peter nodded. Oliver wasn't just his boss but his landlord and flatmate too and he often overheard conversations not intended for his ears.

'I bet that's why he's being such an idiot,' Ian said. 'He's taken on stock he can't move. You know how dangerous that is if he gets busted...'

'Watch out,' Peter said.

Oliver was coming back their way.

'I need to head out,' Oliver said. 'Can I trust you both not to break anything else while I'm gone?'

'Sure,' Peter said.

Ian remained silent, his eyes following Oliver as he passed through the backroom door. 'I'd rather be one man down on a busy Saturday night than have him around.'

'Same,' Peter said as he got up to serve someone new.

They soon did get busy and didn't have a chance to speak again until after midnight when the U-Bahn stopped running. Around then, anyone who couldn't walk home from downtown rushed out with glasses half full to catch the last tram. With only a couple of groups left in the pub, Ian dragged a stool over and Peter pulled them both a small beer. As usual, Ian picked up their previous conversation as if the seven hours in between had never happened.

'If he's ordering coke online it's because he's getting it cheaper that way than he does from his usual suppliers, whoever they are. I bet he's trying to undercut them. Probably thinks he's outsmarting them but if he's using the Silk Road then all his potential buyers are too! Anyone can get on there. There's no mystery to it.'

Peter took a gulp of beer. The bubbles got stuck in his oesophagus. 'Not everyone knows how to get on the Silk Road,' he said with a hand over his mouth. 'I wouldn't.'

'If you did coke you would.' Ian smacked him on the back. 'You just need a Tor. Give me your phone. I'll show you.'

'Er, no thanks.'

'It's nothing illegal.'

Peter pulled out his phone, an older model, but it did the job. He opened it and handed it over.

'You on Instagram?' Ian asked.

'What?' On the way over from the park, he'd looked Markus Mayer up online, found his company website and then very briefly checked him out on Instagram. Peter went to take the phone back but Ian turned with it in his hand.

'I didn't have you for the Instagram type.'

'I'm not, really. I was just checking out places in Stuttgart, you know, bars and stuff.'

'Where's this place?' Ian turned the phone around. The photo he held up was of Markus and the blonde woman and it was on Markus Mayer's page.

'It's Stranded, a beach bar downtown.'

'Jesus. It looks like Marbella!'

'I know. Here.' Peter took the phone from him and quickly clicked on the hashtag for the bar, which got him off Markus Mayer's page. He didn't want Ian to scroll up and see he had purposely gone there. Ian would ask who Markus was and Peter wasn't sure what he'd say. He could tell him a friend said his company was hiring but it wouldn't explain why Peter was looking at bare-chested photos of the guy on Instagram. A photo of the beach bar came up with the Mercedes star behind it and he showed that one to Ian instead. 'Here you go. Just checking places out.'

Ian whistled. 'How much is Oliver paying you these days? I thought he had you on a mini-job wage because of the free room and board.'

'I only had a beer there.'

Peter scrolled down, searching for another panorama shot to distract Ian, but his hand stopped. The next photo on the Stranded account took him by surprise.

'Great to welcome Markus Mayer and friends to Stranded today!'

It was the photo he'd accidentally bombed.

Beneath it, Markus's was the first comment.

'Fantastic afternoon at Stranded. Great drinks and service. Surrounded by so many good friends!'

'Is that you?' Ian asked.

Peter looked at his own face staring back at him – smooth, relaxed, his eyes obscured by sunglasses. It was him but he looked like another person – or rather the same person with another personality inside. Gone was the uncertainty, the twitch that sometimes made his smile crooked.

'Oh, you poser! That's you, isn't it? I'd recognise that ugly mug anywhere. And who are these two?'

'Just a couple of people I met there.'

'Yeah? She's hot.'

Someone was waiting to be served and Peter pushed the phone back into his pocket and took the order. He turned around, grabbed two glasses from the shelf and stuck them under the tap, acting perfectly normally although his mind was reeling.

Seeing that photo of himself and Markus had been like watching the Irish Pub through the reflection in the mirror at the back of the bar. It was familiar but offered a different perspective. Maybe Tina was right. Markus might have been happy to talk about the openings with him. Peter sighed loudly.

'You all right, mate?' Ian asked.

'Just thinking about stuff.' Peter shook his head looking for an excuse. 'Oliver stuff.'

'He's an idiot!'

'I know,' Peter said and turned back to the customer and his own thoughts.

If he'd seen the photo and read the comment earlier while he had been at Stranded he might have had the guts to introduce himself but it was too late. It wasn't as if he could go back there and see Markus again. For one thing, how would he know when Markus was there? For another, how would he afford it? Including the twenty Tina had just given him for a taxi, Peter had about twenty-five euros to his name until payday and that was three weeks away. He handed over the drinks and took payment. By the time he'd given the man his change an idea had begun to take shape.

It was a little after midnight and things were starting to wind down.

'If you want to get off,' he said to Ian, 'I can stay and close up.'

'Seriously? It means you riding home with Oliver.'

'It's OK,' Peter said. 'It's a Saturday night and you've got a girlfriend.'

'Well, if you're sure.' Ian unclipped his server's pouch. 'Cheers.'

Peter wasn't sure but he at least had to try.

CHAPTER THREE

Oliver's small cherry-red Smart was parked up behind a skip and as his boss got in Peter saw the chassis drop. He shifted the printer paper box he'd been given to carry on to his hip, got in and they darted off down the dark but not deserted city streets.

'So,' Oliver said, 'If I lend you this money how and when are you going to pay it back?'

'I don't know the exact date but it'll be from my first paycheque.' Peter moved the box on his knee. The contact with his bare skin made him sweat and he wished it were already cool enough to wear jeans. 'As I said, I need to get a suit for the interview, and if I get the job—'

'If all that stood between anyone and a company job right now was a suit, Suits You would be opening more stores.' Oliver laughed and a gummy smile cracked across his chubby face.

Oliver was right, but he didn't want to buy a suit. What Peter really wanted was the kind of pocket money that meant he could go wherever Markus went and have the opportunity to introduce himself.

'What company is it anyway?'

'Philips,' Peter said. It was a big name here and did a lot of business in English so it was believable.

'And who told you they were hiring?'

'A friend.'

'Can the friend guarantee you'll get the job?'

'She doesn't work there. She just knows about it.'

'A woman?' Oliver ran his tongue over his teeth. 'You mean, your sugar mummy?'

'She's not my sugar mummy, just an acquaintance, someone who interviewed me once.' Oliver had seen him with Tina at a bar downtown. It was shortly after they had slept together, and the look of amusement that had crossed his face had made Peter's skin crawl. 'She's certain I'd be able to get it.'

'I wonder why when she didn't want to hire you.'

Oliver sped up going down the hill. The dip made Peter's stomach lift.

'And if she's so sure, why doesn't she lend you the cash for a suit?'

'Because she's not my *sugar mummy*.'

Oliver shook his head. 'Sorry Peter. I'm not going to lend you a couple of hundred euros. I might be able to offer you something else...'

Peter knew what Oliver was going to suggest.

'I'll front you ten grammes until Friday if you think you can get it sold. Ten grammes for four hundred euros. Charge five hundred and you'll make a hundred euros off that.' Oliver turned the small steering wheel sharply and they drove bumpily over the intersection full of tram tracks. 'Within a couple of weeks you'll be able to buy a suit, a cheap one at least.'

Peter pulled the seatbelt away from his neck. 'I'm not a drug dealer...'

'There's nothing to be afraid of Peter. It's just coke. Everybody does it and it's impossible to get caught. Just don't sell any to the police!' Oliver laughed. 'Seriously, just don't. There's a way to do it. Hint and wait to be asked. The police can't ask you for it. That's entrapment.'

'I don't think that's true.'

'That's my only offer. Take it or leave it.'

Peter bit down into his lip. He really didn't want to sell coke. He'd never be a politician but it didn't matter. What if he sold to someone who worked at Mayer Company and then after he got a job there had to sit in a meeting with them? There was something so explicit about the label, drug dealer. No one trusted a drug dealer even if they were the customer. It was the kind of small indiscretion that might kill his future career. Peter pressed a hand to his forehead. But it was stupid that so little cash stood between him and a decent job. Maybe he did know someone who would buy it from him.

'OK,' he said. 'I'll take it and... thank you.'

Oliver glanced his way. He did a double take almost as if he couldn't believe Peter had agreed. 'Good,' he said and turned the corner.

The electric car hissed up the mild incline and St Elizabeth's Church loomed over them in all its gingerbread glory. At the zebra crossing, they cornered sharply onto Vogelsangstraße, where Oliver had inherited an apartment in a pre-war *Altbau* from a great aunt. The building façade was heavy with oriel windows and a carved doorframe like a tiny palace but inside it was run down. They found a tight parking space behind a new VW California and reversed in sideways.

'Now,' Oliver said, pulling up the handbrake. 'Ten grammes for four hundred euros, by Friday. Deal?' He held his hand out.

Peter reached over the box in his lap and reluctantly clasped Oliver's meaty paw. Oliver's hand was damp with sweat but Peter only realised this after he let go and tried to open the car door. The plastic handle slipped out of his grasp sending the door flying towards the paintwork on the VW and Peter lurched after it. As he overreached the box fell from his knee. Peter fumbled for it but still it hit the floor and the lid came off.

'Damn it! I'm sorry.'

He got out and picked up the cardboard lid, scrambled round to catch the escaping paper and then saw there was something else inside too. Six almost perfectly round, fist-sized white balls wrapped in plastic sat at the bottom. From them came the smell of astringent.

Oliver was next to him now, looming over him and pulling at his belt buckle where it cut into his fat stomach. 'Quick,' he snapped, glancing over his shoulder. 'Pick it up. It's not entrapment if the police catch you standing over six kilos of the stuff!'

Peter replaced the papers and with his heart thumping and hands shaking he fitted the lid, careful to avoid leaving any fingerprints.

AMANDA PERACCHI

Amanda Peracchi pursued a varied career as an English Literature lecturer in adult education; performing arts producer; national director at Arts Council England and cultural fundraising director and consultant. In 2017 she retrained as a secondary English teacher with Teach First and now teaches in a London school.

amandarigali@hotmail.com

An Off-Cut Murder

CHAPTER ONE – A VIGIL AT BONIFACE MANSIONS

In the second-floor flat in Boniface Mansions, Beryl Bridgens sat as close as she could to Cecil Ducat, careful not to disturb further his already outraged body. The dim light of the November morning failed to penetrate the heavy sitting room curtains; a few shafts from the kitchen windows lent a faint aura to Cecil's crushed skull, his brilliantined grey hair made thick with blood and brain. He lay face down, his arms outstretched towards the mantelpiece, as if pleading with the silver-framed photo of a Coronation-robed Queen Elizabeth.

Beryl had followed through for Cecil, had rung the police, but she knew that help for her friend was not going to come from his much-revered Establishment. It was likely to turn its back on him in death just as it had in life, choosing to condemn his minor infringements while expecting from him a lifetime of loyal service.

Beryl sat stiffly upright in Cecil's reading chair, all her energy focused for now on not intervening, not yet. Her strong, reddened hands lay folded in her lap. She wore her work overalls, ready to start the fire and prepare breakfast. Now she felt like a greyhound on a leash, held back from chasing her quarry. Wait. Wait.

'Reminds me of Penshurst, Cess,' she said, her voice finally breaking through the suffocating silence. 'Do you remember poor old Dora, '43? Tried your best to get manslaughter, but the Powers That Be wouldn't have it. Worst luck for her. Managed to fight him off, came out alive. Didn't realise he was a JP. Not something that had come up in their encounter. Once the police found her, it was all over. Civil disobedience, they said. Couldn't go around killing Justices of the Peace, just because they got a bit fruity. Fruity? Almost had her head off, I saw the scar. Did my best, gave her my rations – bar of Fry's chocolate, that was her last meal. Sat up with her the night before. Talked about her mum, promised I'd go to see her. Tried to, but her mum wasn't having any of it. Said that her daughter had died the minute she'd stopped behaving proper. I stayed for the hanging. They told me I should leave, like I had to be shielded from death. Me, shielded! Lost my husband, bombed out my home, stopped more girls topping themselves than I care to remember. Silly buggers.'

Beryl lovingly reached out a hand over Cecil Ducat's body like a benediction. His clothes lent a note of primary-colour gaiety to the tragic scene: burgundy silk pyjamas underneath an Italian paisley dressing gown. There was something almost doll-like about him, his vulnerable thin frame swamped beneath rich fabrics.

By the side of Cecil's head lay the broken remnants of a vase, one of his prized possessions from a holiday in Greece two years ago. A copy, he had proudly informed her, of one now in a museum. Beryl had never liked it – too dreary, black background, picture of some blind woman on it. She inspected it. It looked to her as if someone had flung the vase at Cecil's head, the sheer force of the action causing both his skull and the vase to crack.

Beryl was sure in her own mind that Cecil had let in his assailant. When she had opened the door she had been puzzled by the fact that the mortice lock was undone. He normally locked up last thing at night, leaving her to open it when she popped downstairs from her attic flat to prepare his breakfast. There were no signs of force used on the door and Beryl hadn't found anything out of place in her brief survey of the flat. Even the bed hadn't yet been slept in, suggesting that this visitor had arrived at a time after Cecil had changed into his pyjamas but before he had settled down for the night.

Beryl stood and surveyed his cluttered sitting room, as if for the last time. Musty leather books covered the side table, dainty porcelain figures perilously perched on shelves, piles of paper in some secret logical order on his desk. So many knick-knacks to dust, she'd always complained.

'But the world is so fascinating, Beryl! You must allow me to find comfort in its random beauty,' Cecil had said, in answer to her daily complaints. '*These fragments I have shored against my ruin*,' he would declare.

She caught sight of his diary on the mantelpiece, its unmistakable dark blue leather and gold-embossed cross catching the weak morning rays. She picked her way over and looked through it. Last night, Friday: Artichoke Club. A chat with his old school chums, probably. What had happened in the witching hour between Cecil returning home from this regular haunt and his murder?

She sighed heavily, as if in response to her dead companion's pleas. 'Leave it with me, Cess, I'll see what I can do.'

Just then Beryl heard a smart rapping on the door and quickly placed the diary back where she had found it. 'Right, I'm off now,' she called out on her way to answer the door, carefully placing her slippered feet between the blood spatters as if playing a macabre game of hopscotch. 'There'll be lots of comings and goings for a few days, coppers putting their size twelve boots all over your lovely carpets. Don't take no notice of them. I'm going to get the girls onto this, see what we can do. We won't let you down, Cess.'

With that promise made to her old friend, Beryl went to admit the police.

CHAPTER TWO – THE PAPER TRAIL

The Artichoke Club was beginning to breathe into life, ready to bear the weight of London's elite gentlemen descending for their weekend revels. Glasses were being polished, carpets cleaned and card decks re-sorted.

Down in the cellar, Pym inspected the stacked crates which proclaimed their contents to be from some of the best suppliers in Europe: Ballantine's Whisky, Gordon's Gin, Chateau Margaux Burgundy. She rubbed her fingers along a couple of labels to double-check that they were stuck on correctly.

'Pamela, where *are* you?'

From upstairs Pym heard something odd in the voice of her employer and the club's owner, Giles Ravenscroft. He was always annoyed in having to seek her out, expecting her to behave like some kind of genie, conveniently invisible for most of the day then appearing instantly at his command. This time there wasn't just annoyance in Ravenscroft's voice – there was fear.

Pym hurried out of the cellar, making sure to lock it behind her. At the top of the stairs she found Ravenscroft pacing outside her office. She was struck by the change in his appearance from only two hours ago when he had sauntered in, every bit the man about town, a checked jacket his sole concession to weekend informality. Now he reminded Pym of Hamlet 'all ungartered': he had removed his jacket and tie, sweat patches had formed under his armpits despite the lack of heat penetrating the basement offices and his normally perfect hair looked as if he had stuck his head into a car wash. He spun round when he heard footsteps.

'Finally! I called – why weren't you in your office? Never mind – get any papers related to Cecil Ducat!'

'What do you mean?' asked Pym, 'In his role as a director, solicitor, or as a member?'

'All of them!' barked Ravenscroft.

Pym easily found the files in her well-ordered office. In order to create room for her many bureaucratic improvements she'd had floor-to-ceiling shelving fitted along the wall behind her desk. Her office had become the brains of the company; its financial, logistical and human intelligence made her indispensable.

Pym took the first set of files into Ravenscroft's room, a bigger and normally brighter office, that benefitted from natural and artificial light entering its large window from the busy Soho street above. Today the curtains were tightly shut as if still following blackout rules. Only the desk lamp was lit, showing her employer slumped over his desk, checking back through his personal diary; its gold cross gave the scene a Caravaggian quality.

'Leave them on my desk,' he growled without looking up.

Pym spent the rest of the afternoon sorting through papers which she brought in stages to Ravenscroft. She despaired to see how he had lain waste to her meticulous filing systems. On reordering them all, she learned that he did not seem to have amended or removed anything.

Finally, she deposited the last of her stash relating to Cecil Ducat's membership in front of Ravenscroft. The desperation emanating from him seemed to have infected his desk spider plant, which was now wilting in sympathy. He had undone a number of shirt buttons and drunk substantial swigs of whisky. When he saw the meagre files Pym brought in, he asked, 'Is that it?'

'Afraid so. Were you looking for anything in particular?'

Ravenscroft looked as if he was trying to snap his brain into gear. 'The files – from the start. Don't tell me Cess still had them?'

Pym didn't at first know what he was referring to. She'd started work four years ago, taking over from a young girl who had done her very best to create as much bureaucratic disorder as possible, safe in the knowledge that she could never be sacked as her father was a high court judge. She had finally left to get married and so released Ravenscroft from his bond of duty. Then, she remembered that a few months after taking over as Secretary, Pym had been visited by Cecil Ducat, carrying a large storage box.

'Present for you,' he had said. 'Now that you're in charge I don't need to house these in my flat anymore. Keep them safe, legal documents. Don't let Giles near them, he'll only mess them up.'

'Let me check one last time,' said Pym. She returned to her office and found the box on the bottom shelf where she had left it all those years ago. She undid its lid and removed two boxes of files, both labelled in Cecil

Ducat's handwriting. The first box, 'Property Documents', seemed to be full of papers relating to the purchase of the premises. The second box contained papers relating to the early directors' meetings in its first two years of operations. Cursory inspection revealed all notes were written by Cecil Ducat, presumably in his role as Company Secretary.

Ravenscroft banged open her door. 'What are you doing? What – have you got them?'

'I was just—'

'Give me those!' He snatched the box from under her and carried it away, clasping it tightly in his arms like a long-lost child.

Later, when Ravenscroft had finally left the building, presumably to tidy himself up before the evening began, Pym snuck into his office and searched around. Despite a thorough inspection, the box was nowhere to be found.

CHAPTER THREE – A VIEW FROM ABOVE

Throughout Saturday morning Beryl had made strategic trips up and down the stairs to pass Cecil Ducat's door as policemen had traipsed in and out. They had tut-tutted to themselves as they gave a running commentary on what they clearly considered to be a den of moral filth. '*Silk* pyjamas, if you please, no flannelette here. Did you see the bookcase? Read *poetry*. Only drank *foreign* coffee in those poncy little cups, wouldn't even get a good mouthful out of them.'

The Inspector deigned to put in a personal appearance later in the afternoon.

The Constable had described Beryl to the Inspector on their way up the stairs. 'His skivvy found him when she went to do for him in the morning, sir, old girl lives upstairs with a couple of darkies, bit touched if you ask me. Wants to know all the gory details, reminds me of that Frenchie in Dickens who sat knitting by the guillotine. From what I can gather, he picked her up in prison during the war.'

'He did no such thing.' Beryl spoke as if in direct response to the Constable, defiant in her eavesdropping. 'We were professional colleagues. I was a prison warden and he was a solicitor to some of our guests. And I crochet.' Beryl stood erect at the stop of the stairs, giving the policemen a shock when they had turned the final corner to see her looming above them.

'My apologies, madam. Inspector Pettigrew, this is Constable Ford. We meant no disrespect, just trying to get our facts in order.' The Inspector spoke with quiet authority. He accepted as his right Beryl's invitation to enter her home where his large presence dominated.

They entered immediately in Beryl's sitting room, the beating heart of her home. Evidence of her crocheting skills lay on every surface, from head rests on the ancient velvet sofa to a runner on the collapsible table. Across into the open plan kitchen area could be glimpsed rainbow-coloured crochet pan holders decorating the cream tiled walls. Beryl offered the Inspector the comfort of the overstuffed leather armchair, which he accepted and proceeded to sink ever deeper into. Constable Ford stood sullenly by the door, having conspicuously not been offered a seat by Beryl.

'Now, Mrs Bridgens,' Inspector Pettigrew continued in his practised friendly manner. 'You've given my men a very full description of how you found Mr Ducat, and I certainly don't want to cause you any further distress. I was just wondering if you could give us any information on any, erm, *guests* that your employer may have had over the past few days?'

Beryl sat across from him on one of her dining chairs, eschewing the sofa as she had not wished to sink low on her old springs in front of her visitors. She considered her answer as she poured tea for the Inspector, deliberately ignoring the Constable who stood behind her. 'Mr Ducat was a very quiet, considerate gentleman, he did not do anything to bring attention to himself or disturb his neighbours and I never had any cause to take note of comings and goings to his flat.'

'I understand,' the Inspector said as he accepted his tea and helped himself to a sultana slice. 'I just wondered whether you happened to see any ladies, or indeed, gentlemen, entering the residence, perhaps later in the evening?' He raised his eyebrows in a knowing way as he spoke, displaying to Beryl all the subtlety of a Victorian music hall artiste.

Beryl remained resolutely ignorant in the face of the Inspector's insinuations. 'Contrary to what your Constable thinks, I am not a nosy neighbour. We keep ourselves to ourselves in Boniface Mansions. I cooked dinner for my paying guests, then settled down to listen to the radio. We were all in bed by ten o'clock.'

'Ah, yes, your... guests. Foreigners, I believe?' said the Inspector. 'Would it be possible for us to have a few words with them?'

'You may, of course, but I should inform you now that they know nothing about what happened in Mr Ducat's flat. They were here with me from Friday afternoon through to Saturday morning, and only went out today to use the library. They're medical students on scholarships here. Very respectable,' Beryl added with a note of defiance.

'Couldn't they have left during the night, when you were asleep?'

'Mr Das and Mr Charan sleep in the bedroom; I sleep here, on the bed-sofa,' Beryl indicated the settee with a nod of her head. 'So no, it would have been impossible for them to leave the flat without me hearing them.' She knew that she had begun to sound defensive, aware that her living arrangements were a little uncommon.

When she had moved into her flat four years ago Beryl had optimised its potential for additional income by renting out the sole bedroom to students, content to claim the sitting room as her chief domain. British students having proven somewhat reluctant to share what was a small room in a tiny flat with an ever-present landlady, she had welcomed in two Indian medical students. Devindra Das and Suni Charan had proven to be conscientious and respectful, bringing with them not only welcome income but warm-spirited camaraderie. She was reluctant to expose them to the glare of the British constabulary but had surmised that this cosy chat was not about checking their alibis, it was about checking out her own.

The Inspector continued to eat his sultana slice, crumbs cascading onto Beryl's newly brushed floor. Realising she could not avoid this meeting, she went across the room and knocked on the bedroom door. 'Dev, Suni, would you mind coming out for a moment? The police would like to ask you some questions.'

The door slowly opened and the two young men stepped out, dressed as if they had just come in from the Arctic. Devindra Das's small frame was padded out with a jumper, cardigan and scarf. Suni Charan, taller and plumper than his friend, wore a smart fitted waistcoat over his shirt, but spoilt the look with matching red gloves and bobble hat. Perhaps I do need to add another bar to the fire, thought Beryl.

The Inspector stood up, brushed off any remaining crumbs from his jacket onto the floor and beckoned to the two students to follow him outside onto the landing. 'Could we have a brief chat outside for a moment, lads.'

Devindra and Suni nodded their heads and headed out the front door. As they did so, Suni smiled briefly at her.

Freed from the restraining influence of his superior officer, the Constable came into his own. He paced by the front door, as if guarding it from any nearby eavesdropper. Beryl kept to her queenly dignity on her chair. She refused to give the Constable the satisfaction of seeing any perturbation on her part.

When the students had returned from their interrogation and the Inspector and Constable had left, Devindra had attempted to brief Beryl on what they had told the police. 'Please don't worry, we were—'

Beryl had cut him off. 'No, Dev, that's not necessary. I know you boys well enough to know that you would have told the truth. That's all you can do.'

Suni acknowledged her words with a small bow.

Later that evening, Beryl prepared a hot dinner for Devindra and Suni. She prided herself on showing them the best of British hospitality, with daily cooked breakfasts and hot evening meals. With the warmed pans secure in the oven she took off her apron and followed her set ritual for making herself presentable. Her fine, waved hair was secured with pins to keep it neat in the wind, her nose powdered and lips rouged. Finally, she put on her smart town coat and hat and placed her compact in her brown leather handbag.

Before she left, Beryl tapped on the bedroom door. 'Dev, Suni, I'm just off for a stroll, dears. Dinner's ready in the oven for you. The butcher had some lovely pork sausages, I've opened a tin of peas, and I know you like your spices so I've added a bit of nutmeg to the mash. Help yourself to as much rhubarb cobbler as you like, there's some evaporated milk in the fridge. I may be back late but I'll make sure to be quiet and not disturb you two, I know you need your sleep.'

She then headed purposefully out through the front door into the enveloping November mist.

CHAPTER FOUR – FRIENDS REUNITED

It felt as if everyone around Beryl was fizzing with excitement as they inched their way closer to the centre of London. The bus was packed with suburban dwellers looking to become the city's night owls. Beryl sat at the back of the bus, stuffed between a young couple arguing over which film they were going to catch in Leicester Square ('I've told you Mavis, I'm not watching a bloody French film, you've always liked *The Three Stooges* before, haven't you?') and a preening middle-aged couple flaunting their prized tickets to see Rex Harrison in *My Fair Lady*. Beryl fought her way off at Piccadilly Circus and headed for the dark warren of Soho streets lurking behind Shaftesbury Avenue. She walked confidently past the noisy pubs and red-lit doorways to subterranean clubs and West End theatres. Passers-by gave her odd looks, but Beryl took no notice of their questioning eyes, walking the streets with the same sense of authority that she had walked the corridors of Penshurst Prison.

Beryl stopped by a tall building that seemed to be leaning away from its neighbouring gaudy nightspots in disapproval. There was nothing to welcome guests, instead it was almost issuing them with a challenge to make their way up the stone front steps to the intimidating black door to read the small brass sign. Beryl made no attempt to seek entrance through the closed door, but instead walked round into the back alley and carefully down the stairs to the basement area where she rapped on a small, grimy window.

'Pym dear, it's Beryl. Are you there? I need a quick word,' she called out as if she had just popped round to ask her neighbour for some spare matches.

After a few minutes a head appeared, preceded by a mass of tightly curled dark hair that almost camouflaged its owner's face.

'What are you doing here?' hissed a flustered voice. 'I told you never to come in opening hours. Go away.'

Pym attempted to pull down the window, but Beryl shot in and grabbed the window herself, prising it even further open.

'Pym,' Beryl whispered loudly as she held the window firmly in place, 'Cess is dead.'

'So?'

Beryl gave a stern glare through the window, which seemed to have the power of an electric current shooting through the sooty air. 'Pym dear,' she repeated slowly and firmly, as if to a recalcitrant child, 'Cess is dead. He was my friend, and he helped our girls. He was an old pal of your owner and he was here last night. I want to know what happened.'

'For God's sake, it's Saturday night, come back Monday morning and we'll talk then!'

'Pym dear, you have two choices. You can either pop out and meet with me tonight, or I can knock on the front door and ask to speak to Mr Ravenscroft. I'm sure he would be very interested to know about our acquaintance.'

'You don't scare me, Beryl! I'm a respectable employee, everyone here knows that.'

'Yes dear, very respectable. Just not always *legal*, are you? I'd hate Mr Ravenscroft to start checking your book entries.'

'All right', said Pym in grudging acquiescence, 'meet me at the Moll House in ten minutes. I'll get Ernie to cover for me.'

'Right you are dear, see you then.' Beryl let go of the window and negotiated her way up the stairs again to the street.

Beryl made her way to Soho Square, stopping at a tiny sliver of a Georgian building, the white plaster filling in between two grey stone biscuits. She pushed through the emerald front door and made her way up the worn bare steps to the third floor.

As she stepped through the red velvet curtained entrance, Beryl saw that the Moll House was thrumming with life and good humour. She edged her way around tightly knit clusters of women, some with heads bent closely to each other, some leaning back in laughter, and claimed a tiny side table near the back.

After a few minutes she spotted Pym making her way past the bar. She removed an old army raincoat as she walked, which revealed a demure black dress with a scalloped collar and long sleeves. Her dark skin was bare of adornment, except for grey pearl earrings that peeped out under her deep black curls.

'Pym dear,' called out Beryl, waving above the throng, 'I'm over here. Can you get my special tea for me? Happy to pay for the drinks, wanted to bag a table first.'

With only the slightest nod of acknowledgement, Pym side-stepped to the bar and walked over to Beryl, carrying a small cafeteria tray with a pint of stout, a mismatched teapot and teacup, a spoon and a small shot of whisky.

'That's two shillings you owe me, I'll have the money now, thanks,' said Pym as she laid the drinks out on the table.

Beryl fished around in her purse for the money, muttering to herself, 'The prices they charge for tea now, I don't know where it's going to end.'

'It's not the tea Beryl, it's the whisky. Surely you'd be better off putting milk in your tea at your age? Keep on hearing your generation banging on about shortages, where'd you get your taste for malt?'

'Well,' Beryl chuckled as she handed over the notes, 'it was often easier to get whisky than it was milk. You know, times being what they were.' She carefully poured herself a cup of black tea, using the spoon to mush the leaves in the strainer at the top of the pot, then finished it off with a generous slug of alcohol. 'Got to have a little treat now and then, it's what gets you through.' Beryl stirred her tea and looked squarely at Pym, who was taking a long draught from her stout. 'Now Pym, this is serious. I want you to listen to me. I know you don't want to get mixed up in anything, but you owe me, and I owe Cess. So you are mixed up, so there.'

Beryl looked around to check that no one was looking in their direction. Satisfied that the surrounding women only had eyes for their companions, she began to talk quietly and quickly. 'Cess was killed sometime last night or early morning. I found him dead on the sitting room floor when I went round. Had his head smashed in; sod had used his favourite vase too.'

Pym carried on sipping her drink as Beryl talked, unwilling to catch her gaze.

'You'd heard already. Ravenscroft told you, didn't he?'

Pym confessed to her employer's strange state during the day although said nothing about his obsessive interest in paperwork.

'I found his diary – he was at the Artichoke Club last night. What happened?'

Pym was silent. Beryl waited for her to formulate her response.

'It was just a regular gathering of the Off-Cuts. Cess arrived at about eight o'clock, Ravenscroft was already there of course. Henry Quillam had turned up earlier, his wife probably chucked him out of the house as soon as she could. Edward Garnet arrived just after Cess. I imagine he'd had to wait to find an opportunity to sneak past his old dragon of a mother.'

'Hmph.' Beryl was unsatisfied with this answer but decided to leave it for the present. 'What time did they leave?'

Pym considered again. 'Ravenscroft didn't leave – well I mean not till the club closed. I left at midnight and he was still there. Quillam left first. Cess and Garnet stayed talking until around tennish. I think they left at around the same time.'

'Right,' said Beryl. 'We've got somewhere to start. Those men have dogged Cess's life since the war. I never delved too much when Cess was alive, it wasn't my place. But now he's dead and we're all he's got.'

'You do realise how loony this is, don't you? You've got to leave this to the police, let them investigate.'

Beryl shook her head. 'But that's just it, they won't. It's too easy for them. As soon as I saw him I knew what would happen. We'd have the police sniffing around for a fancy man. Love a good sex crime, they do. Well I know Cess, and I know that it wasn't a bit of harmless hanky-panky that left him with a bit of Greek vase stuck in his skull. There was pent-up anger unleashed that night. Something had been festering for years, and I want to know what it was.'

'But how can you be sure? He did have the odd dalliance. It's not impossible that some man clubbed him for... for – well, I'm not sure what for, but you know, there could have been some reason.'

'Cess had all the hot-blooded passion of Eeyore, and you know it,' snapped Beryl. 'He had gentlemen friends, and I'm not saying they didn't find their way to the bedroom. But he was a talker, he loved the company. Used to play them his record collection, chat about books. I'd get dinner ready for them sometimes. I mean you don't ask for a suet pudding if you're expecting a busy night, do you? Anyway, if it is a sex crime, then the police'll sort it. But we both know that what the police won't do is dig around the Off-Cuts, not unless they have a bloody good reason to, and we're going to give it to them, tied up in a big pink bow.' Beryl sat back, lighting up their corner with her Cheshire cat grin.

Pym sank her head in her hands and groaned. 'Oh God, this is going to be awful. They're going to crucify us.'

Beryl looked down at her in sympathy, this fragile representative of the younger generation who'd only had to live through one world war. 'Oh well, dear, better get another round of drinks in then.'

PAUL STONE

Paul Stone studied Modern Languages at Bristol University, then enjoyed a long career in strategy consulting. He has worked around the world, and now lives in Stockholm. He has a wife, two children and a dog. *Number One* is his second novel.

psto4764@yahoo.co.uk

Number One

Context

Dodgy lawyer, Philip, and his assistant, Danny, an ambitious young Londoner, have just made a deal. They will sell a mansion in Notting Hill to a dissolute oligarch or a corrupt Chinese politician and steal the proceeds. The owner of the house is Philip's client, Robert Smith. He has disappeared, suspected of fraud. As a result, Philip is in trouble with veteran gangsters Archie and Gus. Danny doesn't know about Philip's problem, and Philip doesn't know that Danny is in trouble with the same men.

CHAPTER NINE (ABRIDGED)

Danny

I spotted Stripe giving me the deadeye from halfway down the Portobello Road. I was feeling pretty good until I saw him. I was still on a high from my deal with Philip, and now this. But then, I figured, I'd have to see Stripe anyway, so why not now? Maybe all the pieces were being rolled into place.

He was leaning against the lamp post at the corner of my street. Jez and Big were by his side, hanging around. Waiting for me. They all stared as I came towards them. I didn't break stride. I didn't offer to bump when I stopped in front of them. Big gave me his Big look; Jez looked away.

'Business slow?' I said.

Stripe cleared his throat and spat a slimy green gob on the pavement. He stared into me, trying to psych me out. When that didn't do it for him, he reached forward and took the sleeve of my jacket, rubbing it between his finger and thumb.

'Dat's da thing, you,' he said. 'Why you always wearing my clothes?'

'Maybe because we're on the same team?'

He dropped my sleeve. 'Dat what you think?'

'Don't matter what I think. That's what Gus thinks.'

He nodded his head and a smile crossed his face. Big watched him, his beady little eyes sinking into his flesh like beans disappearing into a thick brown stew. I glanced at his pocket – no sign of a blade.

Stripe sucked his teeth. 'Yeah, Danny. Dat old man… he ain't the only game in town, y'know.'

'He's the only game for you, you got any sense.'

'We'll see.' Stripe stuck out his fist and Big bumped it like a dutiful dog.

I snorted. 'What you gonna do, go over to the Albanians?'

Stripe blanked me, though I could see it hurt to be called on his bullshit. 'You think you in thick with da bossman, eh? One day, he gonna be gone. Maybe dat day not far away.'

'You're fucking nuts. I want to talk to him.'

'You did that already.'

'I got a proposition for him.'

Stripe grunted, shaking his head. 'Yeah, sure. Come on. Let's hear it.'

'Not for you. For Gus. He said, I want to contact him, I come through you.'

Stripe's look turned mean. 'I ain't his fucking postboy.'

I pushed past him and headed for the flat. As I went, I called over my shoulder, 'Yeah, you are. That's exactly what you are. Just another Deliveroo rider.'

My phone buzzed before I was even awake. 06.45. Looked like a pay per go. One message: *You wanna hook up?* Was I getting a Grindr date with London's top hood? I texted back: *Your place or mine?* I had to wait until I was out the shower before I saw the reply. *Bluebird Cafe. King's Road. 12.* Not so bad: I might even live till the end of the day.

I got there early and ordered a coffee. I sat in the Courtyard in a beige garden sofa and enjoyed the steady stream of skinny babes arriving for lunch. None of them quite matched up to Natalia, but there were some on the way. Most of them arrived with carrier bags. They sat and poked at quinoa salads and fifteen quid burgers, and every so often I'd catch one of them checking me out and wonder what she might be up to that afternoon.

I'd just finished my coffee when I heard a blast from a car horn. Gus's Merc was pulled up by the kerb. He was staring straight ahead. I joined him in the car. He set off at once and made the next right and drove round the block. We ended up back on the Kings Road, headed the other way – towards Sloane Square.

Like the day before, it seemed like he needed to get himself on track before he would talk. Or maybe it was another way of psyching me out? If it was, it was doing the job. There's nothing like silence to kick off the sweats.

When we'd settled in, shuffling along behind a gold Roller with Qatari plates, he finally spoke. 'What do you want?'

'I want to do a deal.'

'What kind of deal?'

I took a breath and then let it go. 'I want to buy myself out. Me and Jez. And my family.'

It took him by surprise. He glanced at me quickly, then made the next left. He pulled up by the side of the road as soon as he could. A residents' parking bay.

'You'll get done,' I said.

He tapped a plastic card holder stuck to the windscreen. 'Got a permit. Don't worry about me.'

'Handy.'

'Very. What do you mean, *buy yourself out?*'

'Well... That's what I mean. It's a business transaction. I want to pay you to let me off the hook. I don't work for you, neither does Jez, and we all stay alive including our families.'

He stared at me grimly and I soon got the message he was looking for *why*.

'I'm not your man,' I said. 'I'd be no good for you – this ain't my thing.'

'That's my decision.'

'I'm just saying – you don't want to make a bad hire. It ain't good business.'

'I'm willing to take the risk. All you're doing now is proving me right.'

'How?'

'It takes some fucking balls to come to me like this! I've made people suffer for far less.'

'Why would you do that? I've told you I'll pay!'

'You can't put a price on silence.'

This was starting out worse than I expected. It was almost as though he was deliberately trying *not* to make sense. But then, maybe, that was what I'd let him do.

'Right!' I said. 'I understand – that's part of the deal! My fault. I should've been clear: I'll stay quiet. Nothing ever happened between us. I never met you. Don't know you at all!'

Gus checked the mirrors. Then he looked back at me. 'How much are we talking?'

'I... I don't know. I was thinking a hundred thousand...'

'No. Try ten times that.'

'A million? Shit! Why?'

'Income stream. I know what this business is worth.'

He watched me intently. I tried to hold his gaze. I was getting into a staring contest with a fucking great shark – and I wasn't gonna win.

'I don't know...' I said. 'I'm not sure I can get hold of that much.'

'Where's the money coming from?'

'What does that matter?'

Gus leaned into me and gave me a look that told me it mattered, it mattered very much – to him, and to me. He seemed to grow bigger, there in the car.

'Inheritance,' I said. 'An uncle. He died last week. Left me something in his will.'

'An uncle?' Gus shook his head. 'How much did he leave you?'

'I don't know. He was supposed to be rich... I gotta go away. Meet the lawyer.'

'Where?'

'Caribbean. British Virgin Islands.'

Gus sat back. He didn't stop his staring, but something in his eyes changed. Like he'd suddenly got hungry – like the shark'd picked up a faint smell of blood.

'All right,' he said. 'Go get your money. But leave it there. Get it in a bank. We'll talk when you're back.'

Philip

My meeting with Mr Hung did not begin well. It took ten minutes for his absurd limousine to squeeze through the archway; the driver had to shunt it millimetrically back and forth to navigate the turn into Lavender Square.

The car's rear end was still wedged perilously close to a wall, while its front still endangered a cast-iron lamp post, when Tan hopped out. He strode towards me wearing a single-breasted suit, the colour of which can only be described as some form of puce.

'I hope this is worth it!' he said. 'Mr Hung was compelled to defer a critical meeting with your Minister of Trade to accommodate your timing!'

'I'm sorry, Mr Tan. I thought the objective was to get this done fast? I am sure Mr Hung will appreciate this.' I turned and gestured towards *Number*

One, my hand sweeping wide to convey its full breadth.

Tan stood back and his attitude changed. His eyes fastened upon the blue plaque. 'He'll like that! How much?'

I coughed. 'We are listening to offers above eighty million pounds.'

Tan stared at me, his eyes wide. 'That's perfect!' he said.

'It's a long way above Mr Hung's budget...'

Tan smiled. 'Budgets are made to be broken.'

Mr Hung's gravity seemed undisturbed by his experience in the archway. His entourage clustered around him as he stared at the façade – the same two lads, flexing their muscles, the same two young ladies, displaying their charms. Mr Hung pointed at the plaque and uttered some words.

I didn't wait for the translation. 'Lord Arthur Bashford. A great trader of the Victorian era.'

Mr Hung's eyes did not light up, but I took it from the minutest stiffening of his back that this information was warmly received.

'Shall we?' I said.

We proceeded into the entrance hall, and Mr Hung's eyes were drawn to the giant sculptural light fitting overhead.

'That, of course, can be changed,' I said.

'No need,' said Tan. 'I can see that he likes it.'

Mr Hung also admired the grand central drawing room. If a slight quickening of pace, a raising of the palms and a nod of the head could signify ecstasy, Mr Hung was in heaven. I began to feel a quickening of my heart. As we continued our tour, I started to recognise the signs of his joy. Every new revelation seemed to bring an escalation. Standing at the very edge of the swimming pool, he even mimed a dive, raising his arms into a feeble triangle and turning his head to nod at the young lady of undefined role. She smiled back at him and mimicked his gesture and, giggling, pretended to unbutton her shirt.

When we returned to the entrance hall, my mobile rang. I took it from my pocket and looked at the screen. 'My apologies,' I said. 'I have to take this. Please, why don't you continue to the first floor?' As Mr Hung and his party climbed the staircase, I went outside to answer the call.

My ear was met by a furious voice. 'Do you always hang up on your clients?'

'I apologise, Mr Prostoschutko. I was on the train, the connection was bad.'

'The train? *Bozhe moi!* You English are supposed to have class! Eighty million is absurd. We'll pay seventy.'

'Mr Prostoschutko, I have sounded out the market. Everyone agrees, eighty million pounds is a very fair price...' I had done no such thing – *everyone* in this case was myself and Danny – but I was acquiring a taste for this kind of negotiation.

'Seventy million!' said Prostoschutko. 'No more!'

'Perhaps you should see the house?'

'Why should we see it? We just want to buy it.'

'You should know, we have another potential buyer...'

'What?' I thought I heard the sound of something being thrown at the other end of the line. 'How can you have another fucking buyer? Two days ago, the owner did not even want to sell! Are you fucking with me?'

'Believe me, that's the last thought on my mind! The owner insisted, and I always have a roster of interested parties. I am awaiting their offer.' The line went quiet, but I could hear a murmur of conversation in the background. I looked at the gardens. The trees were blossoming and rich with foliage. The sun glinted on the leaves and warmed my face.

'Simpkins?'

'Yes?'

'We agree to eighty million. When can it be done?'

'How about next week?'

'And that is *Number One*. Aptly named, I am sure you'll agree!'

'Mr Hung is besotted,' said Tan. 'He will make an offer.'

'Well, he'd better make it now. That phone call I took? That was a bid at the asking price.'

Tan gripped my arm. 'Are you fucking kidding me? You're working for me!'

I shook my arm free. 'I can't control the vendor! He already had a buyer in mind.'

'Bullshit!' said Tan. 'Wait here!'

He stalked across the lawn towards Mr Hung, who was inspecting a rose bush in one of the beds. The gardens in the Square, I believed, were the pièces de résistance of the entire proposition. That was why I had presented them last. Who would have guessed that being an estate agent could be so much fun? I closed my eyes and raised my face to the sun, and savoured the anticipation of a warm bath of money.

Tan took my arm again, and I shook myself to life. He led me to a position in the shade of a lime tree and murmured into my ear. 'Mr Hung will pay eighty-five million pounds. If you do not accept his offer, I shall personally see to it that those two big guys carve you into chunks and bury you deep under that little bush.'

'It seems I have no alternative.'

Tan smiled and slapped me on the back. 'You've never done business with someone like me before, huh?'

'You have no idea.'

We crossed the lawn to Mr Hung, and we all shook hands. Mr Hung showed no particular pleasure in what seemed to be perceived as his successful transaction. His handshake was upsettingly weak. I wondered how his translator might deal with the word *gazump*, but that was not a concept I would be introducing today.

'May I wish you similar success in your negotiations with the Minister,' I said.

Mr Hung nodded gravely and started away. While he had been selecting his future abode, his driver had managed to extricate the limousine from the constraints of the Square. As we walked together towards the archway, Mr Hung said something to Tan.

'Mr Hung wonders whether it might be possible to widen the arch?' said Tan.

I shook my head in despair. 'Why not just settle for a different car? A vintage Rolls-Royce would certainly fit through there.'

Upon receiving this suggestion, and for the first time, Mr Hung broke into a smile. To my great surprise, he looked rather cute.

'What the fuck are you doing out there?'

I turned towards the source of this rude interjection. Gus was standing at the threshold of his building, his fists hanging clenched by his sides.

'I'm enjoying the sun.'

'Get inside!' He grabbed my arm and practically threw me into the lobby.

'Steady on, Gus! I arrived early. The Square is beautiful at this time of year...'

'Amateurs!' he said. He swept his card across the reader and pushed me through the security barrier and into the lift. 'This better be important. Archie's in a hurry.'

'I don't need long.'

Sebastian was lounging in a couch in the reception area. His T-shirt and jeans were stretched tautly across his muscular body. The scent of his cologne hung thick in the air. I thought about greeting him, but he gave me a glare and went back to his phone. Gus propelled me into Archie's office, and shut the door with a bang.

Archie was standing before a full-length mirror, adjusting his bow tie. He was in full dinner dress – patent leather shoes, cummerbund and all. 'Sit down, Philip,' he said. 'Apologies for the rush. I'm due at the Guildhall by seven o'clock.'

'Anything interesting?'

'Civic reception of the high and mighty. All the arseholes in town'll be there.'

I sat in the chair before Archie's desk and looked up at Gus. He was wearing his customary leather jacket. 'Are you not invited?'

'Fuck off!' he said. He went around the desk and stood by the window where he could see me.

Archie completed his fine alterations, then turned and spread his arms. 'What do you think?'

'Quite the model citizen!' I said.

'That I am, Philip. That is what I am!' He took his seat, looked at his Rolex and clasped his hands in his lap. His face hardened. 'Ten minutes. What do you want?'

'Well, it's not what *I* want... or rather... This is a courtesy call. I want to inform you that I need to go away for a week.'

'You're a free man. Go where you want.'

'Mr Rumbelow, I'm fully aware that you can track my movements. I would hate for you to become... anxious.'

'Where are you going?'

'It's not really *where* that's of interest to you...'

Gus stiffened slightly and glanced at his boss.

'Forgive me! What I mean is, the important thing is, *why*.'

Archie sucked his teeth. 'All right. *Why*? You got a lead on that shit, Robert Smith?'

'No! No, I'm afraid I can't find him at all. But I may have a lead on some of his money – and that's what you want.'

'I want both.'

'Well, but... you did say *or*...'

Archie glared at me. 'What's the lead?'

'An asset to which – I believe, in the circumstances – I may be able to gain access.'

'An *asset*?'

'Yes. A... financial... instrument.'

Archie looked up at Gus. Gus shrugged. Archie leaned forward, his elbows on the desk. 'What kind of financial instrument?'

'It's... complex. You know Robert!'

'Try me.'

This rather threw me. Despite my hard-learned respect for Archie's talents, I had not expected an interest in the technical details. 'Oh... Well, it's a kind of a Quasi... Derivative... Compound product. It's pretty cutting edge.'

Archie scratched his chin. He glanced again up at Gus. Gus's eyebrows fractionally rose. They seemed to have developed such an acute understanding of each other's body language, that they could correctly interpret shrugs or glances or gestures of any kind based entirely upon the most minute of inflections. I started to become fearful of my own interpretation of this particular exchange.

Archie stared back at me. 'I see,' he said. 'It's a QDC?'

'What? Oh! Yes, I suppose so.'

'What kind? What's it called?'

By now, I was stumped. It seemed I had impulsively discovered a new investment product all on my own. I wondered if this was how Investment Banking worked. 'Ah, yes, it's a Real Estate Backed... Obligation Repossession... ary Vehicle.'

Archie frowned. 'A *REBORV*?'

'If you say so. Does it matter?'

'Yes. That's a risky investment. How much is it worth?'

'Well, I don't know...'

'Have a guess!'

'It depends on the market...'

'For fuck's sake! Stop pissing about!'

'You should get all your money.'

'How much is this fucking *REBORV* worth?'

This was not the path I had wanted to follow, but obviously, that choice was not mine to make. 'I don't know! But I'm pretty sure you'll get your eleven million pounds.'

'Eleven million and forty thousand. And – oh, what a sec...' He cupped his hand to his ear. 'That's the bank just called and the interest rate's gone up – so you can add another sixty k.'

'Fine. That's between you and Robert, nothing to do with me.'

Archie leaned back in his seat. The lines in his face seemed to etch themselves deeper before my very eyes. He scratched at his cheek.

'Where do you need to go?' he said.

I could see it was not an option to avoid this question now. Archie was getting riled and would not be put off.

'The Caribbean,' I said. 'The British Virgin Islands.'

Something passed between the two men. They didn't even look at each other – it was like ESP.

'What is it?' I said.

'Lot a money turning up in the Caribbean these days,' said Archie.

'Always!' I said. 'And some of it's yours.'

'Don't get cheeky.' Archie considered me for a few long seconds, staring grimly into my eyes. He looked at his watch. 'Three minutes. Is there anything else you... need to tell me?'

I shrugged. 'No. No, nothing. I have to go there to access the funds. That's all.'

Archie nodded. 'OK, Philip. If that's how you want it.' He turned to Gus. 'Gus, do me a favour. Ask Sebastian to come in, would you? And tell him to bring the red bag.'

'The red one?' Gus's face was expressionless.

'Yes.'

Gus went and opened the door to the reception area. He issued his instruction.

I heard the reply. 'The red one?' I took it from Sebastian's tone that his spirits were lifted by this particular request.

Gus waited by the door. Archie swivelled from side to side in his chair. He smiled at me pleasantly while I tried not to worry about what the red bag might be. He said nothing. He'd lost his appetite for chat.

After less than thirty seconds, I heard Sebastian enter the office.

'Thank you, Sebastian.' Archie tapped his desk in front of me. 'Put it right there. Close the door, Gus.'

I heard the door close and Sebastian's four quick paces across the room. A red vinyl holdall landed in front of me with an authoritative thump. Archie nodded. Sebastian pulled open zips at each end of the bag, revealing that it was not in fact a holdall, but a kind of rolled-up pouch. He unclasped a strap on the top of the bundle and spread it out across the desk. When I saw what was inside, I sprang from my seat.

Or rather, I *tried* to spring from my seat.

Two great hands grasped my shoulders and thrust me back down. When

I attempted to fight my way out of Gus's grip, Sebastian turned with an air of nonchalance and punched me in the gut. I collapsed instantly. Sebastian dropped to his knees and embraced me roughly, his long reach encircling the chair back, pinning my arms so that I could no longer move from where I was now trapped.

I squirmed, nonetheless. 'What the hell is this, Archie? I'm telling you! I'll get you your money! What the hell...?'

Gus silenced me with a slap across the face.

'Keep quiet, Philip.' Archie spoke softly. 'And stop fucking bullshitting me. QDC? Fucking *REBORV*? Who do you think I am?'

He looked down at the selection of tools arrayed in front of him in the red bag, each of them housed in its own custom pocket. As I followed his gaze, a wave of nausea rose in my throat. Three long knives. A hacksaw. A claw hammer. A steel mallet that I recognised by its serrated surface as a meat tenderiser. A small wooden chopping board and a butcher's cleaver. This toolkit of terror seemed to go on and on. Gus reached past me and pulled something out. He held it up between Archie and me, as if offering wine. A pair of curved and vicious secateurs.

Archie squinted thoughtfully at Gus's suggestion, then to my relief, slowly shook his head. 'Nah. Don't wanna get blood on my togs. Pliers.'

'No! Archie! What have I done? This is a courtesy call! I'm playing the game!'

'Shut it up.' Archie took the pliers from Gus.

Gus clasped a great palm across my mouth. Archie came slowly around the desk, flexing the pliers deliberatively in his hand. My breathing shallowed. My heart pumped fast. The room started swimming as I watched his approach. Gus removed his palm and I gasped with relief.

'Archie! Stop! What is it you want?'

'I already said.' He looked down at me, as if from the heavens, then nodded at Gus.

Gus snatched my wrist and pulled my left hand forward over the desk. As if he'd been rehearsed in some satanic choreography, Sebastian simultaneously adjusted his grasp. He moved his right arm from over my left to a new position around my ribs. He quickly relinked his hands behind my back and forced his head into the side of my face. The stench of his cologne made me gasp.

Gus slapped my hand down onto the desktop, firmly pinning it. All ten of his fingers were wrapped around my wrist. Either of Gus or Sebastian alone could have certainly overwhelmed me. Both together was an invincible force. I didn't even try to fight my way out.

I did try to talk. 'Archie, come on! What is it you want?'

But Archie was miles away, in deep concentration. He stared at my hand, down on the desk, now hidden from me by Gus's broad back. Archie repositioned the pliers, so he now held them downwards in a stabbing inclination. He raised them for a second, as I was still trying to talk him out of his task. Then he moved.

He pressed in close to Gus. He thrust the pliers down towards my hand. He peeled my little finger off of the desk. He pulled it up, and then came the cold, hard touch of the tool. Its jaws bit down onto my middle knuckle, but just as I thought it was going to be crushed, the pressure relaxed.

For a pitiful second, I thought it was over and I began to imagine myself rather tough. Archie was simply adjusting his grip. He pulled backwards sharply, wrenching my finger out of its socket.

It was a strange experience. At first, the only thing that hurt was the patch of flesh that was gripped by the tool. Then came a split-second *lifting away* – no pain, just a sensation that something in my body was being oddly misplaced. The pain seemed to follow as if as an afterthought. And then I was crying and shouting at the walls. 'Christ! Oh, Christ! God!' and all that.

Archie stood back from his handiwork. 'Shut up, Philip. This is nothing. Wait till we get to the thumb.'

Gus shifted momentarily, and I caught sight of my hand. My finger was still attached, but it was standing up at a horrible angle. The pain had risen to an incessant, pulsing thump.

Archie tapped the pliers against his cheek. 'How much is that fucking *REBORV* worth?'

Gus snorted a kind of a laugh. 'REBORV! Fuck!' Sebastian giggled into my ear.

'OK!' I said. 'Twenty... maybe thirty million. It has to be sold before I know for sure...'

Archie frowned at me. Then he turned abruptly to the desk and pushed close in again to Gus's side. He knocked my dislocated digit out of the way, sending a sharp jolt of pain up my arm, and grabbed my fourth finger. When he jerked it with the pliers, I heard a sharp crack.

'That one's snapped,' said Gus.

'Good!' said Archie.

Sebastian turned his head as if eager to see the damage and smeared his cologne under my nose. He received in response a stream of saliva and snot in his hair, as I panted and gasped and moaned in the chair.

'How much IS IT WORTH?' said Archie.

'Fifty! OK! Fifty million! Stop, for God's sake!'

'I'll stop when I'm convinced you've stopped your bollocks. What is this fucking REBORV?'

'It's a financial... thing! Like a bond or something... how the hell should I know?'

Archie went back to work. My middle finger was particularly tough. It took him two attempts to break it. By the end of that, my whole world was pain. Archie tapped the pliers against my shattered fingers. He stood back to view the results of his labour and turned towards me.

'The truth now Philip, or this will go on. Seb and Gus will take you to the workshop. They can do this all night.'

I started to sob. I was a mess. I didn't dare to look at my hand, but I could feel that the blood had drained from my face. A deathly chill scuttered across me and I prickled with sweat. I coughed on the bile that had risen into my throat and blurted out my confession. 'All right! It's a house. A bloody great house! Robert owns it. I helped him buy it. I'm going to sell it for eighty million pounds. There's your money.'

Gus turned and stared at me. Sebastian's grip relaxed on my chest.

My sight recovered to find Archie's expression changed. He waved the pliers at me. 'You said fifty.'

'There's a loan secured on the property. Thirty million. It has to be paid off before the house can be sold. Jesus Christ!'

Archie looked at his watch. 'I gotta go. Gus!' He gestured for Gus to release me and put the pliers down on the desk. 'Philip, I wanna see that house. Eight tomorrow morning. Give Sebastian the address. Seb, darling, clean up this mess.' He collected an overcoat from a cupboard in the wall and put it on over his black tie. 'And dress Philip's hand. It's all right, Philip, Sebastian's very good. Used to be a paramedic – he was attracted by the blood.'

This gave them a laugh. I refused to join in.

'Shall I give him an Alvedon?' said Sebastian.

'Yeah, sure. And one of those yellow ones. And give him some extra – that hand's gonna hurt. Gus, let's go. Philip... This wasn't personal. This is my business. But I fucking enjoy it – and if you ever show me such disrespect again, I'll put those pliers to work on your balls. So, remember now – eight o'clock sharp!'

He patted me on the shoulder as he went from the room.

EMMA STYLES

Emma Styles writes fiction inspired by the remote places of Western Australia where she grew up. Her voice-driven crime thrillers explore young women transgressors looking for ways back, ways through or ways out. Emma has worked as a veterinarian, track-work rider and meditation teacher. She lives in London but always has a bag packed.

emmastyleswrites@gmail.com

No Country for Girls

The highway is long and flat and arrow-straight, running into the setting sun, and that is how he gets into difficulty. That, and his too-frequent glances between the rear-view mirror and the holdall on the passenger seat. A ghost-limbed tree out of blackened scrub, half a painted truck tyre, and a steer, outlined in gold, standing across the centre white line. These things appear suddenly, as static objects, as if he has blinked too long and leapfrogged a section of road.

He brakes, swerves, slews from this lane across into the other.

A lucky escape, to be told loud and with relief to strangers in the pub, the steer moving only its eyes as he passes. If not for the other car.

Afterwards, in the immediate aftermath of the accident and everything that unfolds from it, he thinks of the treasure as his; of this not entirely honest bounty as the making of him as a man.

Here is a country that is there for the taking, after all.

GEENA: RECKLESS

I suck in a lungful of ciggie and hold in the burn, shooting stars through my veins and into every cell to the roots of my hair, and I let it out real slow. The sun magicked itself down so fast I'm stood at Daryl's kitchen window in the dark.

My outline in the black window is like the negative of a photo, the key in my hand sparking like a dollar coin in the light from the kettle. *Woman at kitchen sink, smoking.* The sea breeze late in, pushing cool air and cicada sound through the fly screen, up under my hair and onto my neck and rattling dead bougainvillea sticks against the fence. Bougainvillea is impossible to kill but no one told Daryl that.

He's been gone twenty minutes but he won't find her. She'll stick on the back streets where it's dark and walk the whole way home. It'll take her an hour, maybe even longer, she's only got her thongs on her feet.

Daryl's place is temporary, let's be clear. More temporary than he knows. It's not even a real backyard out there, is it? It's dirt-black sand with his fuck-off new shed taking up half, and let's not dwell too hard on what's been happening in that shed. It's like living in the bush when he's not in the bush, is he? He's in the city? I don't see why he can't plant something. A ground cover, something hardy?

Shit, I'm doing it again; every sentence going up at the end like a question? Even while I'm thinking I can hear myself doing it? Since Daryl's pointed it out, I realise I do it the whole time. I suck in another starburst of smoke and, as he's not here to watch, I trickle it out my nose the way he hates. *Not ladylike, darl.*

Not ladylike, darl, most likely includes having a brain and using it. Daryl doesn't know the half of what's not ladylike, and that's what worries me. Because he's not going to be real happy when he finds out.

My hand shakes and I spill ash into the sink. Let's not get ahead of ourselves, Geena.

I run the ciggie under the kitchen tap and slam-dunk it into the trash, and I take the key down the brick-paved path to the shed. Clear sky and the Southern Cross and my heels *clop, clopping* the pavers to match my heartbeat, too fast and then faster, ramping up to Code Red when next door's sensor light kicks on. There's something wrong with the sensor and Daryl's had words but they haven't fixed it.

The key scrapes loud in the padlock and sticks. I almost bail but the lock clunks open, I rip a nail and suck on a bead of blood. That's two nails down today that I've gotta fix. I'm expecting his fingers in my hair or pinched into the top of my arm to spin me around and ask what the actual fuck I'm doing in his shed.

But, chill. He's not here. I scrape the door over the poured concrete floor. I don't flick the light switch in case the neighbours see it. I can make out the safe, easy; the light from next door cuts a path dead-set to it. A metal box on its side with a neat black square where the door should be, smaller than I imagined it. Daryl's welding gear stacked back on the shelf behind it; the Darth Vader mask and his tools.

It makes it real, seeing it. Safecracker Daryl. Hells bloody bells, what have I started?

I *clop, clop* towards the metal box, slowing down and bending as I get close, scoping the back-corner window for light and the sound of the ute but it's too soon.

Where's the bag? The leather holdall he said was inside? I scout the floor and his shelves of eBay junk and it takes me a too-long moment to realise it's not anywhere, that the dark inside of the safe is empty.

He's taken it with him. Shit. He's driving around in his ute with a stash of stolen stuff in a bag because he doesn't trust me not to take off with it while he's gone? He's that paranoid that he thinks I'm going to double-cross him?

I am going to double-cross him. That stash is for Charlie and me. I just haven't got to that part yet.

I lock the shed back up and take the mobile and my bag and my ciggies into the lounge, and I sit on his fake leather couch in the dark and slide my heels off. The street's quiet out front, my toes digging the cool carpet. A set of headlights scrapes the wall and the bench press and the scratched glass coffee table but it won't be him.

He can't have clocked on. Charlie's got him jumpy, that's all, because she swiped that bit of gold out of his jacket and took off home. I need her to pull her head in or she'll screw up the plan.

Easier said than done. Look at what she did Friday at school; bashing that poor boy's tooth out and getting herself expelled. Not her finest moment, although no doubt she had her reasons. Not the greatest timing, either. She's got a radar for drama, hasn't she? It's her sun in Leo, worst luck. I try her mobile again. Five rings and she picks up. 'I'm not giving it back so you can get fucked.'

I pick a flake of gloss off my lip and breathe. 'Howdy, sis! How's it going with ya?' I say, bright as I can manage. 'Where are you?'

'As if I'm gunna tell you that. Dickhead there with you, is he?'

'No.'

'Got me on speaker so he can listen in?'

'No, I do not. He's not here.' *He's out in his ute looking for you. He's mad as a box of snakes.* 'You could bring it back while he's still out?'

'Fuck off.'

'Chrissakes, Charlie. It's not yours.'

'Fucksakes, Geen! You're not Mum.'

'Yeah, and you're not twelve years old no more!'

She gives that the silent treatment it deserves, and I drop my head to my hand and pinch the top of my nose, thumb and first finger. But that's the exact spit of Mum and when I clock it I let it go.

'Soz,' I say. 'Sorry. Come around here, OK? Get the bus and I can drop you back. I'll tell him you didn't mean to take it.'

'I did mean to fucken take it. Shoulda been more careful with it, shouldn't he? Got no cash for the bus, anyhow.'

Shit. 'Payday tomorrow,' I say. 'OK? I can get some dollars to you, for food and stuff.'

She sniffs. 'What's going on, Geen?'

'I'm trying to get you to bring Daryl's—'

'No, I mean, what the fuck? Whatcha doing at his place all the time? When are you coming home?'

'Soon.' There's rainbow lorikeet racket in the background of the call, the reception in and out like she's talking to me from her back pocket. 'Where are you?' I say.

'Karrakatta. I'm almost—'

'The cemetery? How many times have I told you not to—'

'Keep yer head on. I'm almost home, aren't I?'

'Just be careful, OK?'

There's this queasy ache at the back of my heart, like everything's about to go to shit, only it hasn't started to yet.

'You haven't shown it to anyone, have you?' I say. 'Because—'

'Course not.'

'You can't try and sell it or anything.'

'Because Dickhead Daryl stole it, ya mean? I'm not fucken stupid. How'd he get a hold of it, anyhow? Did he take it from the shop?'

'No! Hell, no. Nothing like that.' But it's close, too close for comfort, and I put her on speaker and light up another ciggie, shaky hands. I blow the smoke away from the screen as if she can smell it.

Loud parrot sounds, her end of the call. 'You reckon it's fake?'

'Fake?' I scratch at my hairline, tight with worry, and a strand of hair catches my broken nail.

It's not fake. There's a whole bag where that one came from. There's a beat where I think I could let her in on the plan, but I don't.

'A scam,' she says. 'That'd be more like Daryl. I like the feel of it, but. How heavy it is. I don't wanna give it back.'

I touch a fingertip to the puffiness under each eye. I need to fix that before he gets back, sort my hair, get some dinner on, suck up a bit. 'Do us a favour?' I say. 'Can you not wind him up any more than you already have? Daryl's not some Year Eleven kid at school, so if he comes around—'

'If he comes around, I'm not gunna let him in. I'm gunna tell him to fuck off.'

I sigh a stream of smoke at the dark ceiling. 'OK. Just don't show it to anyone. I'll see you tomorrow. I'll come around after work.'

She hangs up and I stare at the screen, lifting more dried flakes of gloss off my lip. I rake through my bag for my mirror, can't find it.

I can calm Daryl down. No problem, hon. I can get it back off her tomorrow. I'll tell him when he gets back.

I lift the bag and shake it. It doesn't sound right. The queasy ache flares up and I tip the lot out onto the couch. I find the mirror and concealer straight up, but the rest of what's there is wrong.

He's been in my bag. My keys are gone. I call Charlie straight back but she doesn't pick up.

Shit. I'm a waste of space of a sister. I can't even get this right. She'd be better off in care, except don't say that; don't ever say that. She'll be eighteen next year and we've got a plan, she just doesn't know about it yet.

Another set of headlights rakes the wall and a tune starts up, the neighbours' music from next door. Australian Crawl, *Reckless*. The hairs on my arms flicker like the candles on a cake.

Mum, are you haunting me? Because now's not a real good time.

CHARLIE: SAY GOODBYE

It's dark except for a half-arsed moon and a few street lights. I come out Karrakatta cemo at the main gate and cross the street at an angle. Got my headphones round my neck, music off – I'm not fucken stupid, Geen – and Daryl's bit of gold in my hand, pushed deep in the pocket of my shorts. My thongs going *scrape, slap, scrape, slap* on warm bitumen, some traffic noise off of Thomas Street. There's a strong euc smell off the trees like summer's already here.

A few more streets and I turn into ours, stick my music and my headphones back on. *Reckless*, one of Mum's favourites. It's a shit song, but, too fucken slow, so I skip to the next. *Say Goodbye,* Hunters and Collectors.

I get halfway along before I see the fat girl out front of our place – bent over like she's run a race, leaning on the top of the gate. She's got frizzy dark hair in a plait with half a bottlebrush in it, staring at the busted mailbox, the upside-down number seven. I yank my headphones off when I get up to her. 'Who the fuck are you?'

She jerks upright and spins around. Not much older than me, eighteen tops. She's got a swollen cheek on one side like someone's smacked her in the face and she's puffing from her run, her tits wobbling all over the shop. Her eyes slide up and down me, across the dead brown lawn and cracked concrete path to the front door. Place looks dead with no lights in the windows. 'This... number... twenty-seven?' she says.

'What if it is?' The big square villas either side are blazing out light like they're trying to make our shit house disappear up its own backside. My face burns the same as when Sash came to pick us up that first time. 'Fuck all in there to take, if you're planning on robbing it.'

Her mouth opens and nothing comes out and she shuts it again. She keeps up her puffing. She's got these hooded eyes so I can't see her, not properly. She's not white, either. Got some abo in her, a bit or a lot I can't tell. I shove the gold deeper into my shorts, zip it into the hidden pocket.

Don't know her, do I? She could be anyone.

She grabs a hold of the gate again, head down like she's gunna spew.

'Shouldn't run, it's bad for ya,' I say. The music out my headphones sounds tinny and piss-weak and I click it off. 'You asthmatic or some shit? Not gunna die on me, are ya?'

She shakes her head, frowns at my feet in my thongs. She can talk – got no shoes. Designer denim skirt and jacket and half of Kings Park or Karrakatta cemo in her hair. She straightens up again, taller than I thought she was. Hitches her bag up her shoulder, shiny brown leather. 'You do live here?' she says.

'Who wants to know?'

She frowns like it's a whole big effort. 'I don't know you. Do I know you?'

Sounds fucken posh. 'No, mate. You don't know me.'

What is she, a few brain cells short the full set? Doesn't look it, but. Something about her, like a queen, someone flash. Except what's she doing here? Why's she got no shoes?

She limps a step and her eyes slide past me, looking for someone, checking out the street. My neck twitches and I rub the back of it. Turn and check behind me. Nothing.

A siren cracks the dark along Railway Road and she jumps so high I do too. She spins her head and follows the sound, her eyes big and round. The siren dies away and she looks at me. 'I need... I think I need somewhere to go.'

'Not here, you don't. Not being funny.'

'Seriously,' she says. 'I can't stay out here.'

'You on the run or some shit? Who from? Whatcha pick our place for?'

She's sat down on the footpath, no joke, her back against the gate with her feet stuck out in front. She's scratched them up, bad, too. Got half the western suburbs in the bottoms of them – prickles, glass, rocks, the works. She puts a hand up to her head. 'I don't think I can explain right now.' There's blood there, a smear like black paint. Another dark patch on the hem of her skirt. Fucksakes, I'm not babysitting a fat injured person.

I nod my head up the street. 'Hospital's up there. You know the way?'

'No.'

'Yeah you do,' I say. 'Thomas Street. You not from around here?'

No answer.

'Want me to call someone? I can call someone.'

Her eyes shoot open. 'No! Like, I had an accident. In my car. I need to rest, that's all.'

Bullshit. 'Where is it then?'

She blinks.

'The car?' I say. 'You're meant to stay with it. Not leave the scene, yeah?'

She takes a breath, gets herself back up on her feet. 'Not the hospital. I'm fine.'

There's a Band-Aid on the side of her hand, blood soaking through that too. She's not fine. 'Home, then,' I say. 'Where d'ya live?'

She pulls the twigs and shit out her hair and tries to smooth it down. 'All I want is a couch. Is that so hard?' She smiles like she's making a real big effort, except it only half works. Talks flash, too, seeing as she looks like shit. I don't trust it.

'What, crash at mine? Why can't ya go home?'

'Too far to walk.' Her eyes skitter away like two bugs.

She's lying, it's written all over. Takes one to know one. But I dunno if that gold's real or fake yet, do I? Dunno if I'm gunna be able to sell it or not. Dunno when Geen's coming home.

'Orright,' I say. 'But I need money. Cash in hand, yeah? Forty bucks for the couch, one night.'

She stares at me hard, presses her lips together. Rakes around in her shoulder bag. 'Fine.' She hands over two new twenties, stands back for me to get the gate open.

Fuck. Should've asked her for more.

I push the twenties into my pocket next to my phone. Scrape the gate open and stop there. 'How'd you cut your hand?'

'I told you. I had a car accident.'

I'm not buying it. If she came straight from that where'd she get the Band-Aid? 'You got the keys?'

'What?'

'To the car you stacked.'

A long gap and she says, 'I must have dropped them.'

Yeah right. I'm starting to get this knot in my stomach. 'Not being funny,' I say, 'but if you're gunna be on my couch I think I've got the right.'

She blinks in the light from next door. 'Right?'

'To the full story.'

She presses her lips together and doesn't say shit.

'I do,' I say. 'It's my place and Geen's, and she's away. That's my sister. Don't want to be axe-murdered in my bed, do I?'

'I'm too tired for axe-murdering,' she says. 'But if you want to give me that forty dollars back—'

Bitch. 'Orright.' I'm not gunna think about where she got the forty bucks, what kind of trouble she's in. In the morning she's gunna be gone.

I start up the path and get the key out my pocket – not the one with the cash in, the other one. She tells me her name's Caro, which doesn't mean shit, probably fake. I give her my real one, Charlie. She follows me inside and down the passage to the back. I can smell burnt toast from this morning and it makes my stomach growl. 'You can have the couch in the sleep-out,' I say. 'Not Geen's room 'cause she's coming home.'

Before we get across the kitchen the light in the sleep-out snaps on and I stop, eyes out on stalks and my heart going hell for leather.

Fuck. It's Daryl, the big ugly bastard. 'G'day, Charlize. Been out on the town, have we, you thieving little cunt?'

He's sat in Mum's chair like he owns the place. Back door wide open, Freo Doctor blowing through the screen. 'You're breaking and entering, Daryl. You can get outta that chair, too.'

He doesn't shift, course he doesn't. He's got Bacardi coming off him like kerosene and the bare light-globe above his head is swinging like it knows how mad he makes me. I feel it start in my fingertips, the fucken epi tantrum I'm gunna chuck if he doesn't get out. 'What do you want?' I say. 'Where's Geen?'

'Where do you think? Home making dinner, making herself fragrant.' He stretches his thick neck like he's been practising at the gym.

'This *is* her home.' Makes me wanna puke, the thought of Geen at Daryl's place.

'Not anymore.' He gives me his brick-wall face like he's been practising that too. 'You want my opinion, she won't be back any time soon. Where's my piece of gold, Charlize?'

My fingers twitch towards my pocket but I stop them short. 'It's Charlie, you fat fuck.' A shift of air in the kitchen behind me. Caro. She better stay outta this. 'How'd you get in, anyhow? Better not have busted that door.' I cross the room to the back wall. The lock looks OK and the windows either side are shut.

He opens one hand to show me the keys dangling there. Geen's keys, the Surfers Paradise keyring I gave her. My hands ball into fists and I have to blink. Can't believe she'd send him round here.

He smiles. 'All I want's the gold and I'll be out your way.'

'Too bad. Must have lost it.'

'Don't even try, Charlize.'

'Get outta that chair. You know full well that was Mum's.'

He waggles pink fingers. 'You first.'

The gold burns in my pocket.

Caro calls from the kitchen, 'Where did you say the couch was? I can just—'

'Hold on,' I say to her. 'I'm sorting it.'

Daryl clocks Caro, checks her out like the perv that he is. 'Who's your mate?'

She's propping up the kitchen bench like she's gunna fall down. 'She's not my mate,' I say. 'She needs somewhere to crash.'

He laughs. 'She must be fucken desperate.' He raises his voice to Caro. 'Can't trust this one as far as you can drop-kick her, I'd get out while you can.'

It keeps building, running up through my arms and into my shoulders – how bad I want to punch his lights out. 'I'll drop-kick you if you don't get out my house,' I say.

'I mean it, you little bitch. Where is it?' He stands up and I take two steps back.

'Shouldn't have showed it off to us, should ya?' I say. 'Lost it, like I said.'

Across the kitchen, Caro straightens up.

'I hear your best mate won't talk to you.' He tips his head to one side. 'After you punched out her boyfriend.'

'Shut it, Daryl.' *Don't let him get to ya.*

'No one likes a fighter, Charlize. Not in a girl.' He takes one step and another one, backing me into the kitchen. He's head and thick neck taller and the Bacardi fumes would flatten a camel. 'Like her a bit too much, is that it?'

'Shut it!' I try to count to ten but my eyes are pricking.

'No wonder your sister's left you—'

'She hasn't left me!' I fly at him. It's like hitting a Mack truck with BO.

He grabs the collar of my shirt and slams me into the fridge, back of my head ringing. Geen's keys go flying.

'Ow, you fuck! Watch my headphones.'

'Give me the gold.' Daryl's hand at my neck, twisting my shirt. His other hand groping me down one side.

Caro, behind him – frozen, blinking.

'Fucken perv!' I've got one arm caught behind me and his hand at my neck's like a clamp. I kick his shin but it does fuck all. I go for his face with my nails.

'Bitch!' He squeals and backhands me. I taste blood, but there's a nice werewolf scratch down his cheek. He pins my arm up to the fridge with a fat forearm, tightening his grip on my shirt. He digs in the pocket of my shorts with the other hand, pulls out Caro's twenties. 'What's this? Where is it?'

I smile 'cause he won't find it, but he's twisting the shirt so I can't get air. I'm on tiptoe, fighting for breath, the stuff piled on the fridge clanking like it's gunna come down on us. 'Sold it,' I gasp.

'Bullshit.'

Caro wakes up. 'You're choking her!' Grabs his arm, slips off. Useless.

My feet leave the floor and my mouth opens. I grab the top of the fridge with the arm he's got pinned there, kick up at his nuts and miss.

'Put her *down*.' Caro yanks on his T-shirt. His grip loosens. I get one arm free, scrape at the neck of my shirt. Too tight.

'I'll put her down, all right.'

I grope with the other hand, top of the fridge. What's up there? Wok, breadboard, baking stuff. I hit something – smooth, a long handle.

'Stop! Look at her face.' Caro, still pulling at his shirt.

The T-shirt rips and she falls backwards. Daryl rolls his neck and keeps digging, the other pocket – wrong again.

My lips go numb. My heart's bashing away like a Melbourne Cup loser but I'm fucked if I'm going to. I get one hand around the thing on the fridge and then the other. It's stuck under something, won't shift. I yank and it does, swinging out and down, too quick. Daryl's eyes go massive.

A shit-awful crunch and we go down hard, a twist of arms and slippery sweat and Daryl's big bastard legs. Coloured spots do ballet in my face until I get my fingers to my neck and pull the shirt away, and I choke and cough and breathe until I can. 'Fuck, Daryl,' I say. 'You fucking bastarding fuck.'

It's only then I hear Caro. 'Oh God. Oh Jesus. Oh God,' over and over.

I lift a hand off the floor and I get why. The slippery wet is hot dark red, pooling under Daryl and soaking the top of my shirt.

It's not sweat.

'You could have, like, tried to knock him out with something,' Caro says. 'Not chopped his head in half.'

'As if I meant to!' I'm leant over the sink, retching. Nothing coming out – only spit. 'Didn't know what was up top of the fridge, did I? How about you? Made it a fucksight worse.'

She's bent over in the doorway to the sleep-out, near his legs. I'm not gunna look.

'Not...' I swallow. 'Is he?'

'I'd say so. Come and see.'

I shake my head. 'No way.' I stay at the sink, keep one hand around my throat. I'm shivering, the flanno shirt sticking to me, my blood slowing down, after—

Fuck. Daryl. Geen. Fuck. Don't think about it. I go for the phone on the kitchen bench and punch in the numbers. *You have dialled emergency triple zero. Your call is being connected.* 'Recorded message,' I say to Caro. 'You'd think they'd—'

She's across the room in two steps. Smashes the phone onto the floor and the case cracks open. 'Are you crazy?'

'I was talking on that!'

'You just—'

'Yeah and I didn't mean to! And he might not be... might need a hospital!'

'Wait.' She sticks a flat hand in my face. 'There could still be someone—' She picks up the front part of the phone and listens. 'OK,' she says. 'Dead.'

She looks at me and her eyes go big and she looks at Daryl. I do too and my mouth fills up with spit again. It's like Stephen King – Daryl on the floor with my meat cleaver rammed into the side of his head. Geen gave me that cleaver.

'Thought it was the wok,' I say.

That's what I'll tell the cops. But are they gunna—

There's a choking sound from Caro and I look up. She's got half a fist in her mouth like she's trying not to laugh. Fucken fruitloop.

I rip the phone off her and get the back part off the floor and try to fit them together. 'You've wrecked this. Geen'll be spewing.' I keep trying but it's no good – a bit's cracked off the side and my hands are shaking. 'How can you tell if someone's dead or not?'

'You want to check?'

'No! But what if he isn't?'

'I'll do it.'

I stay hunched over the phone while she does it.

She comes back. 'He's dead. No breathing, no pulse.'

If I didn't know better I'd reckon she was relieved. 'For real?'

'For real.' She climbs onto a stool at the breakfast bar, her good hand curled around the cut one. Must've hurt it, bashing the phone out my hand like she did.

'Still have to call the cops, but, don't I?'

She doesn't answer. She's got her lips pressed together, this thing she does. I see Geen's keys, on the floor by the oven. 'Why don't ya want me to call?' I say. 'What the fuck's going on?'

MARTIN UNGLESS

Martin Ungless has been shortlisted three times for a Debut Dagger, most recently making the Crime Writers' Association's top ten with the opening of *Orange612*. He was awarded an Escalator prize by the National Centre for Writing and has had short story competition success.

martinungless@gmail.com

Orange612

CHAPTER ONE

Cal robs the bank without leaving home. She calls it home, it's temporary. She's doing a handstand with her feet against a column, heels bumping wrought iron rivets as she pushes up and down. She bends her arms then straightens them, counting sets of push-ups whilst waiting for her software to complete.

Seen from here the room is pretty much the same. It's tall, dark, wide and empty, and it smells of cloves. Two windows have had their lowest boards kicked out, allowing moonlight to scrape the dusty floor, as far as the lonely high-backed armchair at the centre, beside the upturned crate. With her body held like this the swathes of moonlight appear to be above her. She looks down – or is that up? – past her body to the sea of space beyond her feet. Black emptiness. She feels like she's flying.

The whole building vibrates. It's a deep throbbing bass which ascends from the basement through the full three floors, because tonight is Student Night at Spice. The music and heat have been rising for hours, so the windows are wide, but the cold stays outside. A bead of perspiration itches on her forehead then peels off, dropping to the floor.

Cal rocks her head back to press it hard against the column so that she can feel the music through her skull. The current vogue is 90s techno, most of it produced before she was even born, but she likes old school. She likes gaming from that era too. She wrote a Tetris for her phone – and sure she gave it nasty habits but that's Cal, seeking out a challenge. Why else would she rob this bank?

Fifteen more push-ups then she's done. She glances over at her netbook. It's balanced on the tea chest and giving off an eerie glow, streams of constantly transforming digits cascading down its screen. Green rain – she likes a filmic reference. As it falls, the digit drizzle passes through a brighter section which remains a line of clear unchanging text, and Cal can read this even upside down, as Orange606. Or could be 909.

While robbing a bank online, if you get the password wrong three times, you'll be locked out, even locked up if you're stupid enough to keep trying in the same place. Cal has a better trick. She takes the same single password and tests it on thousands and thousands of different accounts. The result is that after every failure, when she enters that same rejected password against the next username, and the next, and the next, the bank repeats its simple friendly mantra, 'Welcome back', 'Welcome back', 'Welcome back'.

Cal has a database. She took it when she left. She warned them, and they took no notice. Now it's hers. Account numbers, usernames and birthdates, mothers' maiden names and favourite pets – everything she needs but passwords, which is why she wrote this script. The script tests each new password against her database, 115,211 times.

Orange607.

She bends her arms. With each upwards shove, she forces breath out loudly through her mouth, then as she gently lowers, she breathes in through her nose. The scent of spice is so much stronger near the floor. The music seems to release it from the pitch-pine boards. As well as cloves, she's getting cardamom, nutmeg too, maybe even cinnamon, though that's quite faint.

Up, down, up, down.

Orange608.

Banks add short delays to the login process, customers don't notice, but the wait is designed to thwart blunt force attacks like this. She doesn't mind, she's got 2,048 unique IP addresses running separate logins from a bunch of virtual machines. It's an expensive use of computing power, but Cal's not worried about the cost. Ain't her cloud.

Orange609.

Up, down, up, down.

She pushes through the burn in her shoulders. Up and down. That's thirteen. Up for fourteen, and down. Last push, extra hard. She flips back on her feet. She crouches and swivels to face the chair, then wipes the dirt from her palms on the seat of her baggy cammo trousers. She runs her fingers across her buzz cut hair.

Orange610.

Coffee's not a vitamin, Cal feels ribs through this once white vest, so this week she's being good and trying fruit and veg. Cabbages, bananas, kiwis got her nowhere. The current password being tested is Orange611.

She crosses to the armchair and collapses into it, eyes glazed, facing the green rain. She's slightly out of breath. There's a white flash on the screen as her netbook loads a Customer Welcome page. Cal leans forward, focused, watching her software logging in. It's very elegant. Orange612 is the password, and she's cracked a new account. Her program does everything for her, so already she's inside and using her trackpad to navigate her way to Payments and Transfers. She sits up, drags her phone from a zipped leg pocket, then scrolls through it looking for a suitable account, one of hers, held in a different bank to the one she's stealing from. Here's a balance, £6.27. Not enough for a cash withdrawal, but if she transfers just £13.72...

Cal enters 'Corner Shop' into the Payee Reference box. Who doesn't use them? Banks never check. She takes only small amounts so as not to draw attention, and she doesn't take from those that can't afford. She reviews his recent payments. This mug gave £50 to Barnardo's last week. She's an orphan, he won't mind.

Cal logs out, but her script runs on. She'll stop it in a moment, but first she sits back with a sigh of satisfaction to add this new account and password to her list. The data on her phone is backed up automatically.

In the early months of doing this she quickly picked the low hanging fruit – fools whose password was their birth date, their own name backwards, or even 'password123' – but her progress slowed, so she was forced to write her program. Even with this, the best she can manage these days is to keep pace with replacements for those bastards who change their login details and block her out. She only milks them for drips, to keep it all sustainable, and she rotates through her entire set once every month. This means living off not much more than one small withdrawal each day. She survives, with no rent to pay, and plenty of time to scour the internet for tricks and trades and trouble to keep her entertained.

She's lost quite a few accounts just recently, perhaps the bank sent out a warning email to their customers, so this Orange612 is a real welcome find. She'll celebrate with double coffee in the morning, but right now it's time for sleep, if the party noise permits. It just grew louder.

Cal thinks she's probably tired enough, and tucks her legs up, curling deep into her chair and pulling her coat across her like a blanket. Her coat is everything. Eyes close.

The volume of the music drops again. Cal blinks, stares into the dark. This change in loudness is the ground-floor door to the stair, opening then closing. It's usually someone lost or looking for the toilet. Sometimes they pee on the steps, and sometimes it's a couple going at it, or druggies. She's not a fan. She won't go down, but she listens carefully just in case. The stair is old. She listens because it creaks between the first floor and hers.

Creak. Just like that. And again. Shit. Cal throws off her coat, slaps the netbook shut, and scurries for the darkest corner, furthest from the door.

The door opens, and there's a very dim light coming from down below which reveals the outline of a man. More like a bull, a barrel filling the opening, shoulders rubbing both sides of the frame.

'Out the way,' comes Harvey's nasal voice. Then she sees their shadows do the dance. Harvey's taller, Pugg's so very wide. She thinks most of him is muscle. Their combination, seen in outline – comedy gold.

'You in there, Cal?' says Harvey.

She's pretty sure she can't be seen but wishes for her coat. Its hood pulled forward renders her invisible, invincible, or so it always seems.

Pugg says, 'Come on, Cal, we know you're in here. I saw you come up. What's the deal? Harvey only wants a word.'

Cal wants to be left alone.

'That's right,' says Harvey. 'I'd like to make an offer. We all need money, don't we, Cal?'

She can't see him. It's dark. She says nothing, doesn't move.

'It's just that Pugg here has been telling me what it is you do.'

Pugg doesn't know what she does.

'You know?' Harvey continues. 'A hacker 'n all that.'

Why did she have to get friendly with Pugg? They're in the room now, she hears them moving towards her.

Harvey's saying, 'I could use someone like you, Cal, and you could earn some decent money.'

Cal's silent – listening, peering, and working out exactly where they are.

'I pay well,' says Harvey. 'Don't I, Pugg?'

Pugg grunts.

OK, that fixes their positions. She might even make it between them, out and down the stairs.

Harvey's near the centre of the room.

'Pugg,' he says, 'get back on the door.'

The ox moves to block the exit.

Harvey's facing her, she can tell because she sees the moonlight glinting off his shiny shoes. He's next to the crate. She sees his hands light up as he lifts the netbook screen. Won't do him any good, no one gets in there without a two-part password.

'I don't work for anyone,' says Cal.

Harvey starts towards her.

That's her plan, because she's already moving sideways to the nearest window. Crab-like. She knows it's open, and knows the drop outside is a two full warehouse floors. Nine metres, close on. She knows but doesn't care.

She slots herself into the opening. Cold night air.

Pugg says, 'Here, Cal. No need for that.'

Her toes feel for the edge. She twists, squints back inside, trying to make out Harvey. Pugg's not moved a muscle from the door.

'Come on, Cal,' Pugg calls. 'That's dangerous. Come on back inside.'

She's distracted. Harvey makes his grab. She pulls away and Harvey's grip's not good, the release too sudden. Her foot slips from the sill. She had her weight on it. Her body follows. She's going down. Arms out. Clawing. Falling into nothing. Black below.

CHAPTER TWO

Zed shimmies past the grid of flat screens which cover most of the longest wall. He's a smooth mover, with little pops of arms and legs, bouncing to the rhythm of some funky funky beats which are pumped out by the laptop on his desk. This whole office building is so utterly silent, always so utterly silent, that even built-in speakers feel loud. His desk sits against the short cross-wall, separated from it by the stacks of server boxes – all perforated metal, criss-crossed cables, flashing LEDs. Sometimes Zed imagines the lights are synced to his tunes.

It's a dead dull room, but he's used to it, and the long oblong of oat-coloured carpet is firm underfoot and good for dancing on. The black-painted ceiling's a bit weird, making it hard to see much beyond the cheap suspended lights, and there are no windows. No daylight ever penetrates this chamber, which of course makes little difference when it's the middle of the night.

A bump. Zed twists to see. He thinks the sound was something in the music, a clever use of stereo, that's all. Zed lets go his breath.

He is still bent to look behind himself and he catches his reflection. He's rocking faded jeans and T-shirt and looking pretty hot for someone who's dancing past a big wall of computer screens whilst contorted to peer past a shoulder. Great arse.

Zed turns to face himself fully.

The whole wall opposite is glass and acts like a giant mirror because the room beyond is dark. It's a large open-plan office and never used. Zed pulls some shapes, rides the wave. He smiles. Fit. Got moves. Maybe a little pale from all this never-seeing-the-sun stuff, but his hair is loose, how he likes his curls. He's listening to André 2000, spiky, twisted, fast. Zed eyes his reflection and performs a kind of staccato backwards moonwalk for the full length of the room, laughing when he gets to the end and spins.

The flat screen beside him, nearest to the corner and second up, catches his attention because it's changing. Each display in this gridded wall shows the 'latest statement' from a different bank account, different number, different name. This one happens to be opening a fresh one, after logging out the old. Zed doffs an imaginary cap, impressed by the efficiency. He wrote this script himself.

He scans the statement.

It's not been personalised in over two weeks. These transactions are only the regulars – direct debits, standing orders, mortgage payments, utilities, and the ubiquitous transfer to 'Savings', where the money really goes.

Zed is here to add the personal touches, based on details from the account holder's biography, and these too are brought up by his software, in a small window on the right side of the screen.

He chuckles as he reads, then says, 'Why Mr Johnson, you've been quiet. We both know that can't be true, because really you're a very naughty boy.' He touches the screen to stop it auto-logging out. 'Let's transfer some cash, from...' Zed reads off the neighbouring display. '...from Mrs Jones.' It shows a bank statement in that name. Zed taps the screen to open the Payments window. 'Here we go. Forty quid. Will that cover it?'

Zed writes, 'For services rendered', in the Payee Reference box. He types directly on the screen, all made slightly harder by his constant bouncing to the groove.

'You're so cheap, Johnson.'

Zed hits Submit, then because The Skatalites are playing, he skanks his way the full length of the room and back again.

No need to feel depressed. Everything is going well. His latest plan is working, and just because Maarten wants to see him in the morning, that doesn't make it all bad news. In fact, it's a good sign. Maarten will want changes, and that is precisely what Zed needs. So what if he's fallen behind schedule? It's hardly surprising given everything he's asked to do, by everyone. Zed can fix this. One all-nighter's not a problem. He does without sleep all the time. One or two all-nighters. He grins and sniffs and runs a finger past a nostril. No problem. He'll be done by dawn.

Zed's job is to execute small believable transactions between thousands of different accounts, spread across a range of banks. He's good at it because he makes it fun, and that makes him creative and keeps him going when it's dull. That, plus the need to stay alive.

Zed moves along the wall. A fresh statement. Whoops, he's not been in here for even longer than the last. He spins on the spot, then taps the corner of the screen. He'll buy something from a couple of the Syndicate's take-away accounts. A burger maybe? Not vegetarian are we, Mr Spenser?

Zed spots something.

'Hold on,' he says. He looks uneasily around the room. 'That wasn't me.' He moves closer to the screen. 'Who paid this £13.72?'

The payee reference is 'Corner Shop', just the sort of thing he'd do, but check the timing. His system wouldn't have opened this account again, not if he'd been in earlier today, and it's not like Mr Spenser is out there spending his own money. None of these people are real.

CHAPTER THREE

Cal survived the fall. More than survived. She grins from ear to ear. That was a new move. She wonders where it came from. Not intended. A full turn added to a tomb drop. Big air. She was on the sill, no plan to go face first, the slip was stupid and forced her into a somersault too close to the wall, which made the timing harder for the kick. The kick was perfect. She needed extra strength because of the height she'd lost, but it worked and the rest was casual, a split foot landing, flat roof, shoulder roll to absorb the impact and move her from the edge.

The alley she jumped was only narrow, a beginner's make, though darkness made it hard to spot her two-plant on the asphalt deck. She rubs an ankle. She's crouched behind some metal box – probably an extract duct – one hand down, fingers spread, resting on the gritty surface of the roof. She's breathing hard and trying to contain that grin.

Pugg calls, 'Cal, you OK?'

He won't be able to see her. She's in the moonlight shadow of the taller block next door.

'Cal!'

She knows Pugg can't make out the alley floor. She saw black nothing as she fell.

Her skills surprised her. Sure, she believed that she could do it, or she wouldn't have gone out on the ledge, but she also knew that she was out of practice. She's still fit. What else is there to do? But freerunning is a group activity, and these days Cal moves on her own. She's not made a jump since…

'Cal!'

Pugg sounds so worried, she almost feels like calling out. He's all right is Pugg, even if he does provide the muscle for an avaricious, petty-minded, mendacious, grubby perv.

'Cal!'

Poor Pugg.

Cal hears Harvey. 'Out the way.' They're close. Only one floor up. Harvey's got a hoarseness to his voice, like he thinks he's whispering. 'Move the body,' he says. 'If she's still alive, shift her anyway.'

'Where to?' asks Pugg.

'Somewhere else.'

'Then call the ambulance?'

At least Pugg cares.

'If you want.'

Cal peeks out, still in shadows and reckoning she can't be seen. The moon bathes that whole far wall, so she watches Pugg until his bullet head retreats inside, leaving Harvey leaning out the window, peering down. She could only describe that as a look of disappointment.

She waits until Harvey's gone as well. It's not like she didn't plan for this.

Cal heads away, across the flat roof. She can't see it yet but knows that there's an access ladder on the far edge, down into a courtyard, where the latch to the exit door opens from inside.

Before she descends the ladder, Cal looks back to the old spice warehouse and she sighs. She's enjoyed it there. It's nice and dry, and she never minded the late-night chats with Pugg. She joined him when the crowds had gone, and they talked about Lucy, the kid he never gets to see. Sometimes Emile joined in, whilst he cleared up behind the bar.

Harvey never comes to Spice on Thursdays. She wonders why he's here tonight. The answer won't matter soon, because she's moving on. Her phone and netbook are still inside, but they're both disposable. That doesn't mean there isn't still a problem. Cal's not leaving without her coat.

CHAPTER FOUR

Zed has stopped working on Maarten's bank accounts, though they're still displayed across his wall of screens. Instead, he's sitting at his desk and mulling over what to do about this £13.72. He wonders what it means, and whether he can't turn it to his advantage.

Zed has access to a relay server, this side of the City of London. He shouldn't have the password, but he's going to use it. The server's a connection from a previous job, and he reckons most banking traffic must come through it, for the City at least. Not many people will be accessing their accounts this time of night.

Turns out people just don't sleep. Zed's enquiry produces a massive file. Zed pours through it but it's no good, there are just too many. He pings the bank, then filters using Zebra Bank's IP address.

That's better, not such an endless list. Zed scans quickly, looking for the signs... and this could be it, a transaction from only twenty minutes ago. He runs TraceRoute on the signal. No joy. TraceRoute is going around in circles. It's hit an onion router, probably Tor, which means deliberate disguise, which suggests no accident. But then he knew that.

Who would risk stealing from one of the Syndicate's accounts?

This is his opportunity. He'll tell Maarten in the morning. Meanwhile, he'll set up an alert. People make mistakes, even the sort of people who use Tor.

Or maybe he won't show this to Maarten. If someone has broken in, then they must have information. He could use that, but he'd need to make contact with this someone who is working pretty hard to stay anonymous. He mulls it over.

They must have access to the target bank account.

Zed transfers a further £13.72 from Mr Spenser to the sort code and account number that were described as 'Corner Shop', only he uses a different payee reference. He types instead, 'Z says hi.'

CHAPTER FIVE

Cal waits. She's across the road and down a bit from Spice, and watching the entrance. Cliff-high, above the neons, she can make out the building's original name, Carsten's Oriental Imports, whose metal letters send slanting lamplit shadows across the bumpy surface of the brick.

She got here just in time to see the back of Pugg, scratching his head and squeezing those bulldozer shoulders through the big red door. Since he didn't find her body in the alley, maybe he's happy she survived.

A group of girls emerges, screaming with laughter, and presumably come outside to cool down. Cal watches the cloud of steam for a while before she leaves the safety of her hiding place and wanders casually across the street. She smiles and walks past the group to put a heel up against the wall. She's about three paces from the door. Some of the girls are out of breath. She's jealous. It's been a while.

The risk is that Pugg is on duty. She doesn't think it likely, reckons Pugg is running errands for Harvey tonight. She can bluff her way in past Allen or Paul.

It's a rave-themed club night – that description always makes her smile – which means that Cal's outfit isn't out of place. The vest is spot on, and no one will be looking at her boots.

One of the group wobbles, then strays towards her.

Cal says, 'Good night, ain't it?'

'What? Oh, yeah.' The girl has wide eyes, glinting pink neon. 'Loving it!'

Cal says, 'Can't wait to get back inside.'

In the giggling gaggle one girl shoves another, who trips over, but it's all good fun, and once she's climbed back to her feet the chase is on. They all run back towards the entrance, where they're joined by Cal. She muscles her way towards the centre of the group, clinging to the buzzed-up girl. There's yelling and loud laughter. Cal keeps her head low. She turns away as they bundle in past Allen on the door. They bounce along the corridor, pushing off the walls, more so as they take the corner. After that, Cal slips quietly to the side and lets them pass, watching their bubble of fun rumble on down the stair.

A wave of sound floods up from the basement as the girls open both sets of doors, and she knows Allen can hear this but he can't see round the corner, so now's her chance. Private, No Entry. Cal opens the creaky door and holds it open, so the meagre light from the passageway shows up the bottom of the steps. No one there, nothing as far as the first half-landing. Cal enters the stairwell and the door swings shut. She listens in the dark but that's a waste of time because her ears are overwhelmed by all that boom-fat bass. Cal smiles and bobs, her shoulders rock, and her hands come up in front of her to make small shapes.

Cal starts to climb.

There really is no light in here, she's dealing in shades of black. She's forced to feel with the toe of her boot for every step.

She shuffles round the turning on the first floor and bumps into something soft. Well not so soft, but warm, and wearing a leather jacket.

'Hi, Pugg.'

He grips her arm. 'I'm glad you're OK, Cal.'

'Thanks,' she says.

It's a firm grip. He's got his phone in his other hand, lighting up his face. Serious face. She can see he's texting Harvey.

'Come on Pugg. Loosen up.'

'Harvey'd still like a word, Cal. Why'd you run? He ain't so bad when you get to know him, and that were dangerous, girl.'

'Got scared,' she says. Yeah, right.

The lights come on. She's not seen that before, didn't know they worked. The stair turns out to be a filthy hell.

Harvey appears. Pugg points at the nearest lamp.

'Fuse board,' says Harvey. 'Don't want squatters using my expensive electricity.' He smiles at Cal, then signals Pugg to lead her up the stairs.

There's no resisting.

Cal wonders if she can loosen his grip by flexing her bicep. This only makes the muscle sore.

Harvey's saying, 'I think it's time you got some home comforts up here, Cal. We'll fix it first thing in the morning, won't we, Pugg?'

'Yes, boss.'

'I'd like us to be friends, Cal,' says Harvey.

She doesn't think it's very likely. 'Sounds good.'

Cal wonders where this is going. He's so disgusting, she hopes it's not... How much grease does it take to do that to your hair?

'As you probably know, Cal,' – Harvey's in a chatty mood, more words tonight than ever previously exchanged – 'I've got fingers in a lot of pies.'

'Doesn't sound hygienic.'

'Very good, Cal. Anyway, they're all a bit old-fashioned, these pies. Past their sell-by dates.' Harvey laughs loudly at his own joke. 'Horses, clubs and girls, pubs and... well let's just say, one or two other things.'

'You're a businessman,' she says, meaning out-and-out criminal.

'That's right, Cal, but as we both know, the internet's the future, and I'm expanding. With the right sort of technical knowhow... Pugg tells me you might have those skills.'

'Thanks for that, Pugg,' says Cal.

'That's all right.'

Pugg being so thick is part of what she loves about him.

Harvey asks, 'Why have we stopped?'

'It's broken,' says Pugg. She can hear him breathing hard. For a man his weight, he's climbed a lot of stairs. With the lights on it's possible to see how decayed the steps are up ahead, leading to the top floor.

'Move it, Pugg,' Harvey says. 'We did this half an hour ago in the dark.'

'It's dangerous,' Pugg says. He shifts his grip to Cal's other arm and drops to stand behind her.

She bends then straightens the liberated limb. 'Bleedin' heck, Pugg!'

Cal starts up the final flight. She wonders about tricking Pugg and pretending to put her weight on a piece of wood she knows is soft, but why hurt him when she can just go out the way she did before, only this time with her coat.

'You put those screws through the window frames?' asks Harvey.

Cal twists to see Pugg proudly holding up a screwdriver. She thought hiding in the dark was a bit subtle for him, he must have simply been coming back from screwing shut the sashes.

They've reached the top. Harvey tries the light switch for the room. Nothing doing. It's a cavernous space. It stays dark.

'Damn!' says Harvey. 'Phone, Pugg, phone.'

Pugg lights up the torch on his mobile, and the vague pale circle leads them towards the tea chest. Clicks and echoes come from Harvey's shoes.

As soon as Pugg releases her, Cal grabs her parka and puts it on. She sits because his powerful hands suggest it. She'll miss this armchair. Pugg stands behind.

'Right,' says Harvey. 'Let's have a look at what you're doing.'

The netbook has gone into power saving mode. Harvey waggles his fingers across the keyboard and the green rain starts to fall. He clicks, stabs at the trackpad then tries various combinations of keys. He's not a total Luddite but it gets him nowhere.

'Open it.' Harvey swivels the machine to face her.

Cal doesn't move. Harvey nods at Pugg. She feels his fingers tighten on her shoulder. As soon as she leans forward, Pugg lets go.

She'll do it, but his giving her first access is something Harvey will regret. She keys in only letters. Nothing changes, just green rain. She stops.

'Get on with it,' says Harvey.

She waits two seconds, until of their own accord the tumbling digits all turn blue. Cal types her way back and forth along the top row only, then stops again. She relaxes her hands and leaves them resting on the keyboard. Primed.

As soon as the screen reveals her browser, she presses down on all three keys. The tabs close instantly. The browser's gone.

Harvey grabs the netbook. 'Don't you fuck with me.'

[...]

Pugg's head lies at an awkward angle. He looks uncomfortable. Amazing how people can sleep. From here, when she tilts to the right, she can just make out a strange sharp-cornered shadow on the side of his head. She nears him and sees the colours. Purple. Blue around the edges. Pugg has a square-shaped hollow in his temple. A thin black line emerges from his ear, trickles across the smooth surface of his shoulder, leather jacket, down the sleeve. The black line spreads from cuff to floor. She moves still closer. Understands. Retreats. The single bulb reveals her bootprint to be wet and shiny, red.

'Pugg.' She kicks his leg. 'Pugg, you bastard.'

Pugg does not move.

LUCY WOOD

Lucy Wood studied journalism and had a fifteen-year career as a newspaper reporter and editor before retraining in public relations. She currently works as a PR practitioner and is an editor for a book and magazine publisher. She is a published non-fiction author, and lives in Lincolnshire.

lucyatlincs@aol.com

Holloway

Holloway [hol*low*-way]

A hollow way, a shady sunken track or path, formed by nature, with high banks and a curved canopy of trees, often creating a kaleidoscopic, hypnotic effect on the eye.

At once alive and dead, a holloway conceals and reveals.

CHAPTER ONE

Kit was almost at the kettle when she heard something. She faltered mid-step and stopped fiddling with her dressing gown cord to listen better. Nothing but the dog's meaty breathing, and her own. She shook her head, rebundled herself. The tap spluttered and Wilson started up from his basket, myopic hooded eyes roaming the room. Alarm left him almost immediately and he slumped back down, lids closed.

Moving more quietly, Kit stretched away an interrupted night's sleep. She felt small pops in her joints and relaxed as the ache in her neck eased, a discomfort caused by worn-out pillows she'd been meaning to replace. The kettle juddered to a boil, she tossed a teabag into a mug and poured, no milk, and lit a cigarette, balancing it between her fingers to release the door bolts. A whoosh of air disturbed a stack of papers on the table – work stuff, nothing important – and she rested against the frame, goosebumps puncturing her forearms under the insubstantial dressing gown's fluff.

Standing puddles in the yard had iced over during the night. Gossamer webs looped ornamentally on the hawthorn. Habitually, Kit scanned the perimeter of the yard, once, twice, and was satisfied. It was encouragingly still, and one of those tricksy January days that would con the birds into singing. Winter light was usually dusky and blunt, with rarely a bright morning. Today, though, was breaking with an almost glacial tone, the sky translucent like running water.

She drew on the cigarette and the tip pulsed orange, nicotine sweet on her tongue. Steam spiralled upward from the mug and shimmied in front of her face, dispersing into the dawn. Relishing time by herself, she leaned backward, deliciously faint from holding too long onto the first inhalation. She raised her chin and sniffed the morning. The tang of smoking wood from the fire she'd set in the living room, the muddy scent of the empty hen house, and snow. Snow was coming.

Kit started.

The sound was distinct this time, and unmistakable. The yard gate was swinging, as if someone had just left or just arrived. Her grip on the hot mug loosened. How had she missed that? She ran, leaving the door wide open, ignoring the smash of china as the mug shattered on the step behind her. At the gate she skidded to a stop in flimsy slippers, breathless, and scanned the ground for the padlock. It wasn't there. Careful not to touch, she stepped closer and inspected the electrified cord woven through the bars. It was severed from the power supply. Caught in a gust of wind, the gate swung towards her and she jerked away. Another clang, quieter this time, and there was the padlock, swaying uselessly on the top bar between curled barbwire. It was undamaged, the numbers on the dial set to triple nine, the false combination she always used. And an outsized padlock at that, a warning to would-be rural thieves. Mechanically she pulled the gate towards her, feeling the cold metal bite, and locked it into place. A flock of birds clattered from their roost.

She moved in a circle, scanning the boundary walls for signs of the intruder. There were the same trees, undressed and defiant, and the potholed track leading to the village was empty. The Christmas tree was still toppled by the gate, trailing grubby tinsel and a single silver bauble still attached to a brown spindle. The walls, head-height and capped with a lethal combination of glue and glass. And the gate, the first of a line of defences ritually secured each evening. What the hell was going on?

She recalled the night before, sliding the latch, the satisfying click of the padlock, and the low buzz of electricity feeding the wire. She remembered, so clearly, shooing a sullen Wilson back inside. The old stables had been shut fast and the wood store was undisturbed. Nothing seemed out of place and yet – Kit couldn't make sense of it – there was something, something else not quite right. A throbbing sensation snapped her senses back into place. She unclenched her fist, surprised, as the forgotten cigarette fell to the soil, crushed out of shape. A blister was already blooming in the centre of her dusty palm.

She exhaled and focused, using the pain to tune into the scene in front of her. The farmhouse's cracked roof tiles blushed in the emerging sun, all flaking paint and rough brickwork. The kitchen window was cloudy with condensation, and she could just about make out the shape of flowers on the sill. Blue smoke hung in ropes above the living room chimney and there was a flash of movement as one of the yard cats rounded the corner. It froze and then slunk off, past the closed back door and away, flicking its feral tail.

The closed back door.

Kit ran.

She bore down on the handle, vaguely registering a shard of china digging into the soft sole of her slipper as she lurched over the threshold. Regaining balance, Kit scoured the kitchen to confront whoever had got inside. Wilson was up, growling in her direction. The boiler had coughed on and the room was cloyingly warm, but that was the only change. The sheaf of paperwork was exactly as she'd left it. Her mobile was still charging on the sideboard, an unread message notification making the screen glow. Nothing, and no one. The fright plucking at her innards steadied, then settled into low-level anxiety. The door must have simply swung shut behind her.

The ancient wall clock began its methodical chime of the hour and Kit remained where she was in a tunnel of bitter air, slowing her breathing to match the beats, with no idea of how long she'd been outside. By the eighth strike Wilson was by her side, pressing himself into her legs. A thump sounded from above and his tail wagged. Sunlight pulsed across the kitchen, catching dust orbs in its path and for a long second, she was dazzled.

'What the... woah!'

Kit swung round and lunged in the direction of the voice, not registering that she was reacting at all, only aware of a pulsing sound in her ears and Wilson lumbering under her feet. Encountering the upper body of a man, she pummelled him almost entirely back into the yard.

'It's me! Stop!'

Adam's face was obliterated by dark spots searing her vision. She focused on the starched blue of the uniform underneath his unzipped coat and let her arms hang loose by her side, alive suddenly to how hysterical she must appear.

'What is it?' he said, grasping her elbows within two strides. 'Has something happened to Evelina?' He hesitated, rephrased. 'With Evelina?'

'No, it's not Maw. She's – it's –' Speak Kit, she thought, he'll think you've lost it.

Adam guided her to a chair like he would an invalid and she let him without complaint, thinking of what exactly to say. Wilson bounced stiffly around them, and Adam quietened him with a brief tap behind the ears. He crouched by Kit's knees, and all the urgency had gone from his face.

'Ugh Adam I'm sorry, one sec. Let me sort myself out.' She pulled her dressing gown close, conscious of her threadbare pyjamas, hiding her injured palm in the folds of material and buying time to allow the adrenaline to diminish. 'Someone's vandalised the gate. I think they got in.'

'How? When?' Adam rocked on the balls of his feet. Unbalanced, he was forced to brace himself against Kit's knees. His hands felt gratifyingly sturdy.

'Overnight. The electric wire's been cut and the padlock's moved too.' Her forehead creased, recognising how undramatic the answer sounded, at total odds to the visceral threat she'd sensed out there. Primitive chemicals had instructed her stomach to clench and pupils to dilate. How could she convey what she didn't have the words for?

Adam looked over his shoulder, out to the yard. He was well aware of Maw's obsession with security, ever since the fox culling last spring. She woke up most mornings convinced that burglars had tinkered with the ornaments in her bedroom, or moved the bookmark in her novel to another page, or, on worse days, believing Kit was there to raid the house and hurt her. She'd insisted on endlessly patrolling the house, with Kit padding behind her murmuring reassurances, and then began secreting weapons – knitting needles, a poker, a butter knife – underneath her quilt. It'd taken a downturn in her mobility to put a stop to it, but some of that fear had contaminated Kit or, at least, left a residue. The best way she knew of keeping Maw safe and assured was compulsively to carry out the checks herself, locking them in and everything else out.

Now the angst seemed justified. Someone had got into the yard, surely. Deliberately. Rural thieving was on the up, not that the farm had anything of value anymore, but these gangs were organised and determined, and ready to exploit any sort of vulnerability. The dead end of Christmas had seen a spike in incidents and a leaflet from the local FarmWatch had been circulated, warning residents to be on their guard. How could she explain to Adam what she thought – no, doubted – she'd seen, in the early hours when she should have been sleeping? Not what, but who. An inky form lurking just beyond that damn gate, obscured by nightfall yet a familiar enough outline to make her flesh buzz. Then, as she'd stared harder, the figure lost its contours and became a tree trunk. Nothing more than her overworked brain reordering random shapes. Kit felt fuzzy, as if her skin were draped in a thousand tiny cobwebs, and thought how easy it would be to lose her mind. She pressed her thumb over the blister in the scoop of her palm. That, at least, was something real to hold onto.

'I thought you'd unlocked the gate for me,' said Adam, rising, and glancing at her with an unreadable expression. No more questions, no scrutiny, just acceptance – yet there was no unease either. He thought she was mistaken. There was no intruder. 'I'll look. You stay here, you're freezing.'

He mollified Wilson with another pat on his lemony coat and disappeared, closing the door behind him. His shape passed the windowpane and Kit slouched. She ran through the evening before, recollected smoking a final cigarette in her customary position at the door, dropping the dead butt into the water bucket by the step where it had hissed discreetly, knowing in the morning she'd find it suspended in ice with the rest. She had robotically counted the bolts and locks and latches, a necessary fortification. She'd checked that the timer for the electrified wire was set to switch off just before eight the following morning, in time for Adam's arrival. She remembered – and sensed the prickle of a blush returning to her cheeks – imagining what it'd be like to go to bed with him. Perhaps she'd been more distracted than she realised. Had she really forgotten to lock the gate? She'd been tired – always so tired – so it was possible, she supposed. Doubt began to skulk in the margins. But then, what about the cut wire?

A flicker of the fear she'd sensed outside kindled in her belly and, apprehensive, she unlatched the door. Adam was hunched over the low stone wall dividing the hen house from the rest of the yard, head swinging like a pendulum. He straightened and inhaled so deeply that Kit saw his chest swell. He scanned once more and, seemingly satisfied, strode towards the outhouses.

Behind her Wilson growled. 'I know,' she replied, 'it's raw out and I'm letting it in.' Adam was a charcoal silhouette, moving methodically from one end of the outhouses to the other. A broad man with hefty hands that told lies of his tenderness when it came to Maw's care. So strong, Kit thought, and so very big that he dwarfed any threat by his physicality alone. He could crush as easily as he could care. As if sensing he was being watched, Adam looked directly at Kit, his expression impassive. Then he smiled, gave a thumbs-up and resumed hunting. Hunting, an ugly word she wished she hadn't formed.

There was a familiar clank – Adam must have clipped one of the troughs with his boots – and a huddle of birds emerged from the holloway beyond the boundary wall. They skimmed the treetops and turned left, wheeling out of sight. Even under a blue sky, when wintertime exposed everything within its touch, the holloway remained impenetrable. Kit experienced a fleeting nostalgia for the tomboy child she'd been, then as a teenager desperate for privacy, the bliss of discovering the holloway until...

Kit searched for Adam but couldn't see him. The gate was still closed though, and just beyond it the bumper of his bashed-up old Ford was visible. She shut the door, thinking, flexing her blistered palm, when Adam's shape reappeared, framed by the window. He moved off to the stables, and she observed him rattling each shabby handle in turn. She glanced again to where his car was parked in the lane. Why hadn't she heard him pull up? No car could drive over the old cattle grid quietly. How had he appeared so quickly behind her in the kitchen, when only moments before she'd been running across the yard? Kit frowned, trying to figure out the order of events. She'd been alone as she inspected the gate, and there was no other way in. Did that mean Adam was already in the yard when she'd run out? If that was the case, why hadn't she seen him and, more importantly, why hadn't he seen her or called out her name?

The clock chimed the quarter hour, and then Kit noticed the handprint on the window. She did a double take and without being fully aware of what she was doing, she had one knee on the countertop to get closer. There, in the dead centre of the left diamond pane, was a clear imprint of ungloved adult fingers mashed squarely onto the glass from the outside. The blister burned as her palm connected with the glass, and she adjusted her own fingers to the splayed blur. There was at least an inch to spare around the outline of her own.

The door bowled open, moaning on its hinges. 'All OK,' said Adam, clapping to get warm. 'The cabling has frayed. It's old, that's all, you'll want to be replacing it. There was a broken mug out there, by the way, so I've dumped it in the bin.' He shrugged off his coat and hung it on a peg, paying no attention to Kit clambering down. She watched him ease off his boots and wash at the sink, humming to himself. He rummaged around in a secure box for Maw's medication and clacked his tongue when he found the bottle he wanted.

As easy as that, she thought, to dismiss it all. His attitude was almost cavalier, having failed to see it how she did. What... what if... She considered his stout fingers, surely large enough to match the handprint, and it took strength to fight off the urge to drag him over to the window. He was whistling through his teeth, a tune that had no shape to it. Kit's mind raced through her options. Speak up, or stay silent and observe? Instinct said keep quiet. She'd already behaved erratically enough.

Adam locked the medicine box and reattached the key to his lanyard. He paused, his vast hands resting on the lid. She couldn't help but examine them again, make them fit like a jigsaw.

'Kit?'

She didn't trust herself to speak, so said nothing. She shifted along the counter, blocking the windowpane with her body, testing out the theory that Adam was responsible.

'It's all right, honest,' he said. 'It's fine, apart from being bleedin' freezing. No one's been in.'

'OK.' She spoke slowly, knew there was an edge to it. 'You're saying the wire's gone through old age, fair enough. What about the padlock? Why would that have moved by itself?'

Adam's head jerked at Kit's tone. For a moment he was confused. 'There's nothing wrong with it. Like I said, I thought you'd opened up for me. I figured you must've changed the code.' He began fiddling with his watch strap, an action he seemed to be using to delay the next line. 'It's locked onto the top bar – you must've missed the catch in the dark. There's nothing wrong, there's no damage. Nothing deliberate, anyway.'

Kit reddened. She had gone outside last night without a torch because the moon had been bright enough to see by. But the darkness... he was right about that. It was the kind where anything beyond a few feet stopped existing. And when was the last time she'd checked the cabling on the gate? Well before the dark weather arrived, she was sure of that. She'd set a pile of wood blown down in the autumn gales burning before performing the inspection, and the acrid smell from the ashes had hung around for days. So why did the wire look as if it'd been cut, neatly? Kit was again seized by doubt. The mark on the window was surely indisputable evidence. The intruder had been careless enough to leave a trace. Why would anyone touch the glass unless they were trying to get inside, to break in? And, having got this far, having gone to all that bother, why hadn't they actually done it? Unless. Unless they didn't want to get in – they just wanted to look. All the fire faded from her cheeks. That idea troubled Kit more than anything else.

'...pretty handy yourself, but what with it being live you might be best getting someone in to sort it.'

Kit nodded dumbly, not hearing. She scrutinised his hands, just the right size. But this was Adam, for God's sake. Was this what hysteria felt like?

'Jeez, you're as tense as an over-tuned guitar. You look like you're in shock – actually, you might be in shock. A sugary cuppa, that'll do the trick.' He was babbling. 'Too isolated, this place. Wouldn't catch me living out here, no way. Listen, please. Nothing's wrong.' He emphasised the last two words.

Kit wanted to believe him, desperately, but the evidence said otherwise. She counted up the incidents in her head. The roving padlock, the frayed wire, the handprint. The man she swore she'd seen at three o'clock that morning in the lane. Adam knew about her life, the layout of the house. Perhaps it was cash? Her occupation sometimes involved keeping money in the study safe, and he'd walked in on her once, crouching at the door of the safe. Had it really been accidental? His salary was average, but rents and bills were high, and he couldn't afford a new car. Maybe Adam planned to sneak in and... Kit exhaled. He was looking at her with bemusement. He shrugged, double-checked the lock on the medicine box and drummed on the lid. 'Right then,' he said. 'I'll check on Evelina and set the bath running, then make us a cuppa.'

'You're here early,' Kit replied, folding her arms, eyeing him.

'Actually—' Adam hesitated, blushed. 'I thought I was late.' He waggled his wrist. 'My watch battery's dead, I noticed it on the way over. And you know what the old banger's like, her clock only tells the right time twice a day. So...' He trailed off.

'So.'

'I might have put my foot down a little bit. Not clever in this weather, granted. You've caught me out.' He flung his palms aloft in a you-got-me gesture. 'The roads are so bad round here. Why you insist on being so isolated I don't know.' The joviality sounded artificially bright. 'Anyway, here I am. To help, I mean, and I'm glad.' He risked a glance at Kit. 'Looks like I came just at the right time.'

'Yeah.' Kit gripped onto the countertop behind her back. 'You see, that's what I don't get.'

'What?'

'I don't get what happened just then.'

'Sorry love, you've lost me.'

'How did you get in here,' she gestured to the kitchen with one arm, 'so fast without seeing me in the yard?'

'I did see you. I got out of the car and you were standing there, by the door, with your back to me. I thought you were trying to get Wilson out for a pee.'

'Right,' she said, straightening to full height. 'Right. Only I didn't hear a thing – didn't hear you coming up behind me. Don't you think that's odd?'

'No. I don't.' His voice was flinty, and the warmth was gone from his expression. 'What exactly are you saying?' His jaw performed a little jutting motion. 'Are you accusing me of something? Of doing that out there?' He pulled out a chair and sat down and dragged a palm across his stubble. 'Seriously.'

There was nothing but the ticking of the clock, and Wilson's old-man breathing from where he was curled in his basket.

'Seriously?' It was a question this time. When she didn't react, he seemed disappointed. 'Why don't you sit down.'

Wrong-footed, the rush of adrenaline was gone. What *was* she doing? She'd charged him with trying to break into the house. He leaned his elbows onto the table, waiting for her to sit, and the lanyard – purple, the colour Maw had chosen for herself – swung about his neck. A lanyard that held the duplicate key for the medicine box and obviously, in case of an emergency, a spare key for the door. Obviously. She felt herself go icy cold, then flare hot. What had been an unshakable truth just moments before began to disintegrate. He had no need to break in – he could walk in, at any time, day or night. That was part of his job. What wasn't in his remit was the way he'd dropped everything to search the yard and reassure her, an act of kindness. Humiliation washed over her. Why had it taken so long for the logic to catch up? A terrible thought bubbled in her brain and she wasn't fast enough to quash it. Was early onset dementia, Maw's sort, genetic? She could ask Adam but didn't want to know the answer. She sat, and the surface of the table gulfed between them.

'I think I'm losing it,' she said woodenly.

'No.' Adam stretched out his arms and laid them flat. 'It's perfectly clear what's happening. Don't give me that look, I can see what you're thinking. You're overwrought – nothing more. You're certainly not ill. You've not...' There was a pause. 'You haven't got what Maw's got. Don't go thinking that.'

'You reckon.' Was she so transparent? Through the torrent of thoughts, Kit tried to remember what day it was. Sometimes, the days, weeks, blended into one.

Adam was nodding. 'Seen it all before. You can't be in a job like mine and not recognise the signs. You're a carer too – much more than I am. I come and go, and Evelina isn't my mum. The stress is immense.'

'I don't deny it. It's been rough lately. And—' She broke off and tested a tepid smile. 'It's dreaded tax return time. Busiest time of the year for me, workwise.'

Adam slapped both hands palm-down onto the table with a bang, making Wilson jerk. 'There we go then. There are no intruders trying to pick their way in. You're knackered – no offence. As if you had me pinned as a burglar. I thought accountants were meant to be logical.'

'Oh God,' Kit half laughed, covering her mouth with her good hand. 'How can you be so nice to me?'

'Didn't I just say I've seen all this already? There was this family, right, when I started out. Mum terminal, dad lost both legs to diabetes. Mum turns around and says I nicked her purse. Turns out the eldest lass had it, she'd got on the bus to the supermarket instead of school, to help out. Mum was mortified.'

'Hmm,' Kit nodded. 'Mortified. A bit like me right now, maybe?'

'Don't be daft.' Adam tapped the tabletop. 'Listen, have you run through what you did last night? Can you remember?'

'Yes. I was so sure I'd done everything in order, as usual.' She bit her lip.

'I'm hearing a "but" in there.'

'Yes. I mean, no. I mean, I guess I messed it up. It's just, you know, the farms round here... we're not exactly Fort Knox... the gangs...'

She replayed it all once more, exhausted. The padlock and cabling, fine. The figure at the gate, easy to make shapes from shadows. The handprint. What about that? She risked a fleeting look behind her to the window. It was visible but smudged and ill-defined through the rising condensation, and from where she sat, the angle was different. What had at first seemed like fingers fanned out upwards, in the shape of... a wing. It was exactly the sort of mark left behind by a bird, having had the misfortune to crash-land into glass. The sort of mark that occurred all the time on a farm in the middle of the countryside. A handprint, Kit, as if. Her thoughts had been so exaggerated and hammy lately, so unlike her, that she hardly recognised herself.

'My life!' She wondered if she were coming down with something, if a fever could explain it, and felt around her neck for signs of a temperature. 'This wasn't exactly what I signed up for.'

Adam gave a courteous smile but said nothing. He'd had a run-down of the family history. A father who'd been long-term ill before his death, and a sister permanently absent but with a shiny husband's cash to pay for Adam's salary. Money in exchange for keeping her hands clean and keeping her distance, and a bargain in which Kit had no say. There were no friends to speak of. Adam knew it was just Kit and Maw, in it together, and he'd been there the first time Maw had what he termed an incident – when the disease put on a show of its capabilities. Maw was puzzling over a crossword, concentrating just fine. Then Kit thought she was seeing a ghost – Maw, stripped to her underwear and shoeless, trying to climb into the hen house. The fear of her falling and breaking bones, the fact that she'd slipped from the house without either of them noticing... Adam had lifted her down from the wall with the effort it took to pluck a flower, Maw weeping Pa's name. After that, she became a monochrome version of herself, pared down and insubstantial. Less colourful, as if she'd been faded by the sun. Like she had made a conscious decision to rot.

'No, not the gangs,' said Adam. 'They want combines and quad bikes, and you've said yourself there's nothing here anymore. Anyone, even a city boy like me, can see this isn't a working farm. But maybe, if it'd make you feel better, you could report it?' Kit recalled the FarmWatch leaflet shoved into the dresser drawer. 'But seriously, love, I'm no electrician but I reckon it's a matter of maintenance, and probably a big bill for it n'all. Anyway, I'll just fill Wilson's bowl before I go up to Evelina. His water's run dry.'

Kit spotted the empty bowl and balked. Adam rose. Was that a pointed glance? There were dirty plates in the sink, and crumbs from last night's hastily eaten toast on the tiles. The clothes horse was loaded with charity shop shirts and hand-me-down jeans. She knew what it looked like. Incompetence. That added to her erratic behaviour, to describe it mildly, made her queasy. Adam had managers. He had procedures. What might he say to them? 'The house is a mess. She wasn't washed or dressed when I arrived and she was delusional, saying someone had tried to break in and then accused me too. Potential fantasist here. We need an urgent assessment.' Kit felt a pinch in her stomach. Maw wasn't going anywhere.

'There you go, boy.' Wilson was lapping at the water in the replenished bowl as if he hadn't drunk for days. The traitor. 'Right then, I'll set to running a bath, but Evelina should have breakfast and pills first. Will you be wanting to take it to her?'

'Adam, I...' She halted, unsure of how to say thanks for everything he did for Maw. Thanks for just being there. She was desperate for a cigarette but didn't like to smoke in front of him. It was indecent, somehow, another kind of admission. Instead she reworded herself with a well-rehearsed smile. 'Yes, good plan. Maybe later she'll feel like coming downstairs.' Her face was tight and waxy, the smile pinned on top. She tried one more time. 'I – I mean, thanks. For everything. It's so hard to distinguish fact from fiction out here.'

Adam had the fridge door open, the light from inside changing his profile to the colour of an ice cube. He paused and regarded her, and she knew then it was with pity.

Acknowledgements

This anthology comprises extracts from the novels written by the 2020 cohort of the UEA MA in Creative Writing: Crime Fiction. It has been made possible by the generosity of the UEA School of Literature, Drama and Creative Writing in partnership with Egg Box Publishing.

We would like to thank course directors Henry Sutton and Tom Benn and tutors Julia Crouch and Nathan Ashman for their guidance, support and inspiration. Thank you also to the Crime MA students in the 2019 cohort for making us feel so welcome and supporting us throughout our course.

Over the past two years we have been privileged to receive masterclasses from many exciting and inspirational crime authors. Thank you to John Banville, Erin Kelly, Dreda Say Mitchell, Yrsa Sigurðardóttir, William Shaw and Elly Griffiths for sharing their insights and experiences on writing and publishing crime fiction. We are also grateful to Dr Stephen Day for giving us a stimulating session on forensic science theory and the opportunity to work a 'crime scene'.

We are also grateful to the fantastic team at the National Centre for Writing and to all the amazing authors they bring to *Noirwich* each year.

A huge thank you to Jasmin Kirkbride, Nathan Hamilton and Shannon Clinton-Copeland from the UEA Publishing Project, Emily Benton for her wonderful book design and Sarah Gooderson for her extremely thorough proofreading. Thanks to the editorial team – Mark Hankin, Lin Le Versha, Lissa Pelzer, Emma Styles and Martin Ungless and proofreaders Denise Bennett, Amanda Rigali and Paul Stone.

Thank you to the Norwich pubs and restaurants, particularly the Sir Garnet, The Birdcage and The Murderers, for providing us with the gallons of Prosecco, wine and beer plus the fish and chips required to fuel our creative discussions. We are also grateful to the staff at Broadview Lodge for ordering taxis and making sure we had a good night's sleep.

We are grateful to the Main Scholarship and the Little, Brown Prize for their contribution to budding crime writers.

Finally, we would like to thank our families and friends for their support, patience and encouragement throughout the course – we hope you enjoy reading our work.

UEA MA Creative Writing Anthologies: Crime Fiction

First published by Egg Box Publishing, 2020
Part of the UEA Publishing Project Ltd.

International © retained by individual authors

This book is sold subject to the condition that it shall not, by way of trade or otherwise, be lent, resold, hired out, stored in a retrieval system, or otherwise circulated without the publisher's prior consent in any form of binding or cover other than that in which it is published and without a similar condition including this condition being imposed on the subsequent purchaser.

A CIP record for this book is available from the British Library
Printed and bound in the UK by Imprint Digital

Designed by Emily Benton Book Design
emilybentonbookdesign.co.uk

Proofread by Sarah Gooderson

Distributed by NBN International
10 Thornbury Road
Plymouth
PL6 7PP
+44 (0)1752 202 301
e.cservs@nbninternational.com

ISBN 978-1-913861-04-9